"Sharon Martin's *Cutting Ties with Your Parents* is an indispensable resou͟[ͅ]... difficult decision to sever ties with abusive parents. Martin provides a step-by-step guide to navigating the complex
emotions and practical considerations involved in this courageous choice. This workbook is a road map for
healing and empowerment, but also a beacon of hope for those seeking to reclaim their lives and prioritize their
well-being."

> —**Tracy A. Malone**, best-selling author, international coach specializing in narcissistic
> abuse, and founder of Narcissist Abuse Support

"Sharon Martin's *Cutting Ties with Your Parents* is a helpful workbook and guide for adult children navigating
the challenging journey of detaching from difficult or abusive parental relationships. Martin offers insights and
actionable steps toward healing and reclaiming autonomy, providing essential support for those seeking liberation from familial toxicity."

> —**Mari A. Lee, LMFT**, founder of Growth Counseling, The Counselor's Coach,
> and author of *Facing Heartbreak*

"Sharon Martin has created a masterful and practical gem of a workbook for those cutting ties with their
parents. In this workbook, Sharon has created a clear and direct path toward accepting this decision, so the
reader is left with no stone unturned. Bravo!"

> —**Sherrie Campbell, PhD**, author, podcast host, and clinical pathologist

"There is so little in terms of support for adults who have a difficult relationship with their parents. It's important that people who survive abusive dynamics have a process for protecting themselves. This book adds something really special to the field, and is a strong tool for helping adults decide for themselves how to manage
family relationships."

> —**Becca Bland, DLitt**, specialist coach, researcher in family estrangement, and founder of
> Stand Alone—the only nonprofit for estranged adults

"When we make a brave decision to break the cycle of generational trauma, it can be a lonely journey filled with
confusing thoughts and emotions. In this book, Sharon is inviting us to experience compassion, non-judgment,
and community through her explanations and writing exercises. If you are feeling confused about difficult decisions in your healing journey, I believe this book can bring you comfort and clarity."

> —**Elisabeth Corey, MSW**, founder of www.beatingtrauma.com, and trauma recovery
> life coach

"Cutting ties with parents isn't a decision made lightly. Actually, it's often a last resort after pleas by the adult
child for their parents to understand the impact of the way they were raised have fallen on deaf ears time and
time again. Sharon Martin understands the pain of family estrangement, and compassionately guides those
whose childhoods were unsafe to create relationships that protect them from further harm and
re-traumatization."

> —**Laura Reagan, LCSW-C**, host of the *Therapy Chat Podcast*, and founder of the
> Trauma Therapist Network

Cutting Ties with Your Parents

with Your
Parents

A Workbook to Help Adult Children

Make Peace with Their Decision, Heal Emotional Wounds,

and **Move Forward with Their Lives**

SHARON MARTIN, DSW, LCSW

New Harbinger Publications, Inc.

Publisher's Note

NEW HARBINGER PUBLICATIONS is a registered trademark of New Harbinger Publications, Inc.

New Harbinger Publications is an employee-owned company.

Cover design by Amy Daniel

Acquired by Ryan Buresh

Edited by James Lainsbury

Printed in the United States of America

26   25   24

10   9   8   7   6   5   4   3   2   1   First Printing

Table of Contents

Introduction

If you picked up this book, you've probably cut ties with one or more of your parents—recently or perhaps many years ago—and you're still hurting. You may be wondering if you made the right decision. You may feel guilty, sad, anxious, and angry. You may be struggling to maintain firm boundaries. Or you may feel stuck and not know how to move forward and create a fulfilling life for yourself. Although estrangement and family conflicts are isolating experiences, you are not alone! During my twenty-five years as a therapist, I've worked with numerous adult children who've cut ties with a parent after decades of anguish and mistreatment. I've seen them recover and build fulfilling, satisfying lives—and I know that with support and resources, this is possible for you, too.

Unfortunately, resources for those experiencing family estrangement are sparse, and the social stigma attached to it is strong. Some fear that books such as this one promote estrangement as the solution to all family discord. Rather, this book recognizes that family estrangement is a reality for many; it's a painful experience, and adult children need and deserve support and guidance. I believe—and research supports—that cutting ties can be instrumental in healing from a painful or difficult relationship with a parent (Agllias 2018; Allen and Moore 2017; Scharp and Dorrance Hall 2017).

Who This Workbook Is For

You'll benefit from this book if you're experiencing any of the following:

- You cut ties with one or more of your parents or another close family member and want to heal and move forward with your life.

- You've cut ties with a parent or family member and are second-guessing your decision.

- You've exhausted all efforts to repair your relationship with your parents yet feel guilty or conflicted about cutting ties.

- You've reduced contact with a parent to preserve your well-being and are having difficulty maintaining distance.

- You want to free yourself from controlling, abusive, manipulative, or otherwise harmful parents.

How This Workbook Is Organized

This book has three parts: "Acceptance," "Healing," and "Thriving." In part 1, you'll clarify your reasons for cutting ties, learn how to make peace with your decision, and move forward with the knowledge that you did your best and made the best decision possible in a difficult situation. In part 2, you'll practice effective therapeutic strategies to heal from the effects of family estrangement, including grieving and managing difficult emotions like anger and shame. You'll also learn how to care for yourself in ways your family never did and build a support network to help you heal.

In part 3 you'll explore how you can thrive by living authentically and feeling good about who you are, developing healthy relationships, maintaining boundaries, and coping with holidays and other challenging situations.

How to Get the Most Out of This Workbook

The concepts and therapeutic exercises in this workbook follow a natural progression, so I recommend reading from start to finish. Some chapters may not seem relevant to you, but I encourage you to still read them, as you'll find useful and affirming materials in every chapter.

Written Exercises

Every chapter contains exercises and reflective questions designed to help you gain new insights and progress in accepting, healing, and thriving. Some will be more challenging than others and may bring up difficult emotions and memories. Go at your own pace and treat yourself with compassion throughout the process.

Online Materials

Some of the exercises in this book are available at this book's website, http://www.newharbinger.com/53905. You can print additional copies and repeat them as often as you find helpful. See the back of the book for more details.

Journal

You may also want to use a journal to record thoughts, feelings, challenges, and successes that emerge as you complete this workbook. This will help you integrate what you're learning, process your emotions, and notice your progress.

Therapy

Healing from the effects of family estrangement and recovering from childhood trauma is a complex and difficult process. If you get stuck or discouraged, reach out for help. A therapist or support group can provide additional therapeutic support and coping skills. If you experience increased symptoms of depression, anxiety, or suicidal thoughts, please consult a mental health or medical professional. Mental health resources are listed in the appendix at the back of this book.

Stick with It

Change takes a lot of effort and practice, and people often give up before they've given new ways of thinking, feeling, and behaving the time they need to take hold and be effective. I encourage you to persevere even if you don't see positive changes immediately.

It's a privilege to be able to guide you through this process. I'm confident this workbook will provide invaluable guidance, and your ongoing commitment to healing will keep you moving forward long after you've finished this book. Let's get started!

Part 1

Acceptance

CHAPTER 1

Understanding Your Reasons for Cutting Ties

Juan was newly estranged from his mother when I started seeing him for therapy. As an only child, he felt exceptionally guilty about "abandoning" her. "Tell me a bit about why you cut ties with your mother," I prompted, in an effort to help him come to terms with his decision.

"Her drinking was the biggest problem," he said, with tears in his eyes. "But we've had problems forever. There are so many reasons. I don't know where to start!"

We spent multiple sessions exploring why he ended his relationship with his mother; his reasons were numerous and complex. Not only was his mother unwilling to change her hurtful behavior in the present, but a lifetime of hurt preceded his decision.

For most adult children, the decision to cut ties with a parent is complicated and painful, as it was for Juan. In my experience, most agonize over their decision and often feel guilty, second-guess themselves, and struggle to maintain boundaries—sometimes even years after they cut ties. Some have trouble healing and moving forward because they haven't made peace with their decision. This is understandable. It can be hard to accept that cutting ties was your best option, especially in a world that tells us family relationships are the *most* important relationships.

The chapters in part 1 of this book focus on acceptance because acceptance is a prerequisite for healing. Acceptance helps you to move forward with the knowledge that you did your best and made the best decision possible in a difficult situation. Understanding why you cut ties will give you confidence in your decision and help you to start feeling good about it. Let's start by looking at the most common reasons adult children cut ties with their parents.

Why Adult Children Cut Ties with Their Parents

Some people have a hard time understanding why adult children cut ties with their parents. It goes against conventional expectations that families will stick together no matter what and that the parent-child bond is unbreakable. But the reasons are actually straightforward. Research consistently shows that adult children typically sever ties because they feel mistreated by their parents (Agllias 2016; Carr et al. 2015; Conti 2015; Scharp, Thomas, and Paxman 2015). The following list contains the most common reasons adult children give for cutting ties with their parents. I imagine you can relate to some of them.

- Emotional abuse (manipulating, shaming, blaming, gaslighting, minimizing, or dismissing your feelings and needs)

- Verbal abuse (yelling, name-calling)

- Emotional neglect (indifference, not attending to your feelings and emotional needs)

- Physical abuse

- Sexual abuse

- Not protecting you from abuse perpetrated by someone else or not providing the support you needed

- Betrayal (lying, humiliating you, or gossiping about you)

- Sabotaging or undermining your other relationships

- Controlling or demanding behaviors

- Rejection

- Differing values

Before writing this book, I wanted to explore for myself whether adult children's experiences with cutting ties reflected the research I found. Between November 2022 and June 2023, using my website and social media accounts, I surveyed over nine hundred estranged adult children about their reasons for ceasing contact with one or more parents. My findings were similar to those of other researchers and are shown in figure 1.

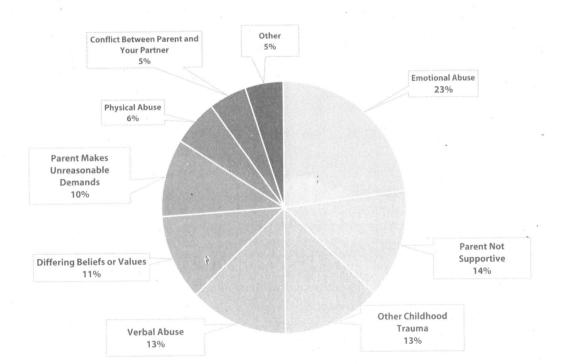

Figure 1: Reasons for Cutting Ties with a Parent

The adult children that I see in my therapy practice cite a combination of present-day issues and harm that occurred during childhood as contributing factors. It's not simply that their parents hurt them or failed to meet their needs in childhood; their parents continue to harm them even after they're grown and living independently. They dismiss their feelings and needs, criticize and demean them, belittle their choices, disparage their identities, violate their boundaries, and make unreasonable demands of them. They fail to see their adult children as separate, capable, and worthwhile people who deserve to be treated with compassion and esteem. Sadly, strangers often garner more respect from these parents. Adult children are hurt further by their parents' refusal to acknowledge that they caused them harm. They won't make a sincere and complete apology, and time has proven that they are not willing or able to change their behavior.

A Decision of Last Resort

No one wants to be estranged from their family. Cutting ties with a parent is a decision of last resort—one you only make when you've exhausted all other options (Agllias 2016; 2018; Scharp 2016; Scharp, Thomas, and Paxman 2015). In over two decades as a therapist, I've yet to encounter anyone who made the decision to cut ties lightly. Adult children typically struggle to resolve their family conflicts for years before calling it quits. They set boundaries only to have them ignored. They sacrifice their mental health and well-being. They give up their goals and values. Sometimes, relationships with their partners and children are damaged by their efforts to please or appease their parents. Only when the pain of continuing the relationship is unbearable and the damage is extensive do they call it quits. There is rarely a single reason or event that causes parent-child estrangement. For most, cutting ties is their final option. It is a painful decision that comes after years of mistreatment and attempts to repair the relationship.

> **Gentle Reminder:** You tried for years to have a functional relationship with your parents before concluding that it's not possible.

A Form of Self-Protection

Cutting ties with a parent is an act of self-protection (Agllias 2018). Adult children don't do it to hurt or punish their parents—although it's often perceived this way. Cutting ties is something you do for yourself. It's an effort to stop hurting, to protect yourself from further pain. Others may misunderstand your decision and try to use it against you. However, please remember, protecting yourself is a healthy choice.

> **Gentle Reminder:** You didn't cut ties to hurt your parents. You did it to safeguard your own well-being.

Safety is a universal human need; everyone needs and deserves to be safe. If you don't feel physically and psychologically safe, it's hard to focus on anything else because so much of your time and energy is spent trying to protect yourself. As a healthy, mature adult, it's your job to take care of yourself—and that begins with keeping yourself safe.

You Aren't Alone

Although estrangement isn't spoken about openly, it's not uncommon. When Richard Conti (2015) researched the prevalence of family estrangement in the US, he concluded that the results "suggest that estrangement is widespread, perhaps nearly as common as divorce in some segments of society" (34). In a US survey conducted by psychologist Karl Pillemer (2020), 27 percent of adults had cut off contact with a family member. Of the 1,300 individuals surveyed, 10 percent were estranged from a parent or child, 8 percent a sibling, and 9 percent an extended family member. The prevalence of family estrangement is similar in the UK; the charity Stand Alone (2014) estimates that one in five British families experience estrangement. In addition, research conducted by Stand Alone and the University of Cambridge (2015) shows that over half of parent-child estrangements are initiated by the adult child, and the majority of adult children who cut ties strongly believe they can never have a functional relationship with the parent from which they're estranged.

I hope that these statistics help you make peace with your decision and feel less alone. There are millions of people experiencing family estrangement, and many of them are adult children who, like you, needed to cut ties with their parents to protect themselves and allow themselves to heal and move forward with their lives.

Adult Children's Stories

The following stories explain the reasons why three adult children—Mina, Juan, and Dan—cut ties with their parents. As you read their stories, take note of what they have in common and how they differ. We'll return to their stories throughout the book.

• *Mina*

Mina, age thirty-two, grew up in Chicago with her parents and two older brothers. Mina describes her family as cold and unloving. There were no hugs or words of comfort. Her father was critical, harsh, and demanding. The entire family walked on eggshells around him, and Mina received the worst of his rage. He routinely called her a whore or a fat cow while she was growing up, and told her she'd never amount to anything. As a result, Mina never felt good about herself. She pushed herself to be perfect to prove her worth and appease her father. She worked hard in school and was devastated when her father told her he wasn't going to pay to send her to college. He had paid for both her brothers to go, but Mina's father dismissed her feelings and goals, saying that women should stay at home and that he wasn't going to waste his money on her education. Mina's mother made excuses for her husband, saying things like, "He's doing his best. You need to stop provoking him." She never stood up for Mina, encouraged her, or consoled her.

Mina knew it wasn't safe to defend herself and that she'd never change her father's mind, so she rarely tried. However, when she became a mother, her tolerance for her father's disrespect dwindled. He continued to call her derogatory names in front of her young daughter despite her requests that he stop. The final straw was her mother feeding her daughter, who has celiac disease, a piece of bread. This wasn't the first time her parents had ignored her instructions; she'd spoken to them numerous times about the importance of her daughter's gluten-free diet. When she confronted her mother, her father stepped in and told her she was overreacting. "She'll be fine! Gluten free is some made-up, new-age bullshit. It's always something with you!"

The following week, Mina tried to talk to her parents about what had happened and asked that her boundaries be respected. Her father rolled his eyes and said, "Get over it." Mina left in tears. After that event she had no contact with her father. Her mother would call occasionally, but only to try to convince her to talk to her father. Neither offered an apology. She heard from her cousins that her parents started bad-mouthing her to the rest of the family, claiming she was mentally ill and threatening to seek custody of her daughter.

• Juan

Juan, age forty-seven, cut ties with his mother eight years ago due in part to her alcohol use. As the only child of a single mother, Juan supported his mother emotionally and financially for years without question. He saw it as his duty—what any good son would do. He paid for some of her bills, chauffeured her around when her license was suspended, and helped her get into treatment programs multiple times. When he married, he realized how dysfunctional his relationship with his mother was. His mother ruined every holiday and family event by getting drunk and doing something that embarrassed him. The next day she was quick with a hug and an apology but never changed her behavior. His mother's neediness also created tension between Juan and his wife; his mother constantly wanted Juan to come over and help her with something or she needed money for rent because she'd lost her job again. Meanwhile, Juan had responsibilities to his wife and children that his mother didn't seem to appreciate.

They had an on-and-off relationship for ten years before he finally cut ties. During this time, Juan tried to set boundaries. He stopped inviting her to family gatherings. Sometimes, she'd show up anyway or she'd complain incessantly about being left out and unloved. He told her to stop calling in the middle of the night unless it was an emergency, but she didn't accept that losing her glasses or needing cigarettes did not constitute an emergency. Juan was distraught about his decision to cut ties with his mother and felt tremendous guilt about leaving her alone. They went to family therapy together, but after his mother came to a session under the influence, the therapist said she needed treatment for her substance use before they could continue. Juan tried one final time to arrange treatment for her, but she refused to go.

Juan went to therapy on his own to try to make peace with his decision. For the first time, he recognized how much effort he'd put into helping his mother only for her to refuse to take any action to improve herself and her situation. He started to grieve all that he'd missed as a child. He'd never been able to play sports or have friends over. He'd struggled unnecessarily in school because his attention deficit disorder was never diagnosed. He'd been the one to cook, clean, and pay the bills. He used to jokingly say that he raised himself. Now, he feels sad—and a bit angry because he shouldn't have had to.

• Dan

Dan, twenty, is a transgender man from South Carolina who's been partially estranged from his mother and stepfather for two years. He learned early on that it wasn't safe to be himself at home. When he was three years old, he told his mother that he wanted to wear a suit, not a dress, to church, and she slapped him across the face. His parents insisted that he wear feminine clothes, take ballet lessons, and try to "pray away the gay." They used threats, guilt trips, and name-calling: You're going to hell. You're an embarrassment to this family. You're a girl and you need to act like it. I can't even look at you. You're disgusting.

During high school, he was kicked out of the house when his mother discovered he was binding his chest. Dan lived on the streets for two weeks before attempting suicide. After a brief hospital stay, he returned home because he didn't have anywhere else to go. Disregarding the hospital social worker's recommendations, his parents refused to use his chosen name and male pronouns. Instead, they made a point of using his dead name repeatedly in every interaction. Dan asked to go to family therapy; his parents said they would, but they never made an appointment despite his repeated requests. Dan grew increasingly depressed.

Eventually, he found solace in an online community of trans people of color. With their support, he channeled his hurt and anger into a plan to leave home. He found a job, saved money, and was accepted to a college in Boston. Leaving home was a relief; he finally felt free to be himself. Dan tried to maintain a relationship with his parents and thought he could tolerate them in small doses. However, when he went home for the holidays, it took him weeks to recover from the mental anguish. His suicidal thoughts returned. He was anxious and couldn't sleep. His grades plummeted. He longed for his parents' acceptance and affection but knew that spending time with them was destroying his mental health. He cut off all contact for a year. Then, he saw them at his grandmother's funeral and decided to try again.

As part of the reconciliation, his parents agreed to call him Dan but then didn't follow through. His mother claimed she couldn't remember to do so, or that it was too hard to change after twenty years. Dan tried to be patient and give her time to adjust. He suggested books and support groups that might help her. She made excuses, which largely consisted of blaming him for ruining the family and insisting he was a sinner who needed to repent. Dan, again, told her how hurtful her behavior was. She ignored his feelings and said she was the one who'd been hurt, not him.

What stood out to you about Mina's, Juan's, and Dan's reasons for cutting ties?

Mina: _____

_____

Juan: _____

_____

Dan: _____

_____

What did you notice about their parents?

Mina: _____

_____

Juan: _____

_____

Dan: _____

_____

What thoughts, feelings, or memories surfaced as you read their stories?

_____

_____

_____

_____

_____

Understanding Your Reasons for Cutting Ties

Now that you're familiar with the most common reasons adult children cut ties with their parents, it's time to focus on _your_ situation and clarify your reasons for cutting ties. There aren't "right" or "wrong" reasons, so try not to judge yours. For now, your goal is only to understand what contributed to your decision to cut ties.

Gentle Reminder: There are probably numerous reasons for your estrangement. You may find it helpful to think of them as layers. The top layer is the final straw, and underneath is a multitude of offenses and unmet needs that, when stacked upon each other, make the relationship intolerable.

Exercise: Reflect on Your Reasons for Cutting Ties

This set of reflective questions is designed to help you gain clarity about your reasons for cutting ties. Take your time answering them. If you feel overwhelmed or upset, take a break and come back to this exercise when you feel ready.

Why did you cut ties with your parents? (Consider recent and childhood occurrences.)

_____

_____

_____

_____

_____

_____

How has your family of origin negatively impacted you?

_____

_____

_____

_____

_____

_____

_____

Was it always this way? When did the difficulties start?

_____

_____

_____

_____

_____

Did you communicate your hurt to your parents and ask them to apologize or change their behavior? If you did, what was the outcome? If you didn't, what got in your way?

_____

_____

_____

_____

_____

_____

_____

Were your parents open to therapy or other treatment services? How did this impact your decision to cut ties?

_____

_____

_____

_____

_____

Did your parents acknowledge and apologize for the harm they caused? Was it a sincere and complete apology? How did this affect your relationship with them?

_____

_____

_____

_____

_____

How did you know you couldn't continue the relationship?

_____

_____

_____

_____

_____

Was cutting ties a form of self-protection or liberation? How so?

_____

_____

_____

_____

_____

_____

What do you think would have happened if you hadn't cut ties?

_____

_____

_____

_____

_____

_____

Final Thoughts

Understanding why you ended your relationship with your parents—and knowing that others have had similar experiences—is a huge step toward accepting your decision and letting go of guilty or ambivalent feelings. In the next chapter, we'll look at why estrangement can be a healthy choice, which will help you feel even more confident about your decision.

CHAPTER 2

Accepting Your Decision to Cut Ties

Accepting your decision to cut ties with your parents means you know it's valid and you feel at peace with your decision. However, acceptance doesn't mean you'll never have doubts. Most people have doubts when making a big decision, such as getting married or changing jobs—and deciding to cut ties or limit contact with a family member is definitely a big decision. So, you may not be able to eliminate all your doubts about your choice, but this chapter will help you feel certain that it was your best option.

Good Decisions Don't Always Feel Good

The pain associated with family estrangement can make it hard to have confidence in your decision to cut ties. It seems like good decisions should feel good, but good or healthy choices don't always feel good when we make them. Take starting a new exercise routine, for example. You know it's good for you, but it's challenging to begin one, and sometimes it's literally painful. It often takes a while for us to realize the benefits of a good decision, as is often the case with distancing yourself from a family member who mistreats you. It's going to hurt for quite a while, but that doesn't mean it was the wrong thing to do. With time and healing, the benefits will likely outnumber the struggles.

> **Gentle Reminder:** It can be painful to make good decisions, and it's common to feel conflicted about them.

Sometimes There Are No Good Options

As the old saying goes, you were stuck between a rock and a hard place. You didn't have any truly good options. You could have continued the relationship with your abusive or controlling family members, knowing it would cause you further harm. Or you could sever ties with them to protect yourself and move forward. But, as a result, you no longer have these family relationships and may feel stigmatized, isolated, and misunderstood. As we covered in chapter 1, no one *wants* to be estranged from their family. This wasn't the outcome you wanted, but given your options, cutting ties was the best choice. If it's hard to see cutting ties as a good decision, you might reframe it as *the best decision in an impossible situation*, or *the less bad option*. Take a moment to reflect on this decision.

What alternatives did you have?

_____

_____

_____

_____

_____

Why didn't you choose another course of action?

_____

_____

_____

_____

Do _you_ believe it's a bad decision, or is someone or something else telling you it's wrong to cut ties?

_____

_____

_____

_____

> **Gentle Reminder:** When you're in an abusive relationship or dealing with a family member who refuses to treat you with dignity and respect, there are no optimal choices.

Trust Yourself

Self-trust is the ability to trust your own perceptions and judgment. When you trust yourself, you have confidence in your decisions even if others disagree. It's often hard for folks who grew up in dysfunctional families to develop self-trust. We develop self-trust as children, when our perceptions and inner experiences match the external world. Here's an example: A child feels hungry and says, "Mama, I'm hungry. My stomach is rumbling." If her mother affirms her hunger, the child will learn to trust her perceptions. However, if her mother says, "You're not hungry. You just ate," the child will not trust her own perceptions and bodily sensations. When this happens repeatedly, children learn that other people's perceptions are right and theirs are wrong. This makes it hard for them to trust that their thoughts, feelings, and choices are valid or correct.

> **Gentle Reminder:** When your parents deny the harm they caused, they undermine your ability to trust yourself.

Family secrets, emotional neglect, gaslighting, lies, and abuse all erode self-trust. In dysfunctional or abusive families, it's common for parents to deny their children's experiences of abuse or maltreatment. They may say it never happened or that the child is overreacting. They may focus on having met their child's physical needs, but not understand or care that failure to meet their emotional needs caused harm. As a result, some adult children aren't sure if they've been abused or mistreated. They blame themselves and minimize their hurt because they've been taught that their perceptions are wrong and their judgment can't be trusted. Undermining your self-trust is a form of manipulation and a tactic to keep you mired in a dependent role or an abusive relationship.

> **Gentle Reminder:** You get to decide what constitutes abuse or harm, not the person who hurt you.

Rebuilding self-trust involves tuning in to your experiences and courageously choosing to believe yourself, even when no one else does. Most of us want validation and approval from others. Our need for other people's approval is hardwired into us; as babies, our survival depends on being accepted into a family group that will care for us. When we get external validation, it's easier to accept our decisions and feel good about them. However, you don't need other people's approval—especially your parents'—to make peace with your decisions; continuing to do so can be harmful. Peace comes from accepting and trusting yourself. It doesn't have anything to do with your parents understanding your decision or acknowledging their role in the estrangement. They will probably never understand your decision. They have proven that they are committed to misunderstanding you and invalidating your feelings and experiences. To make peace with your decision to cut ties and move forward, you must accept that your parents will not provide closure. They will never be a source of comfort or healing. This is a sad truth, but it is the reality for many adult children who cut ties with their parents. Take a moment to reflect on the state of your self-trust.

What makes it difficult for you to trust yourself?

_____

_____

_____

_____

Accepting Your Decision to Cut Ties   19

How have others undermined your ability to trust yourself and have confidence in your perceptions, feelings, and choices?

_____

_____

_____

_____

_____

Validate Yourself

If you have a supportive friend or partner, you may have gotten some validation that's helped soothe your uncertainty or guilt about cutting ties. However, external validation never entirely resolves self-doubt. Confidence in your decision must come from within. Fortunately, you can affirm your own experiences, feelings, and choices, and you can comfort yourself. Doing so can create a powerful shift in your life, from looking to others for validation—and frequently being disappointed that they don't provide it—to trusting and caring for yourself.

Self-trust is also more effective than external validation because you know yourself and your family better than anyone. Only you know:

- What you've been through and what led you to cut ties with your parents

- How their mistreatment has impacted you

- How hard you tried to resolve your family conflicts

- What you need to heal

- What's true for you

Exercise: Self-Trust Affirmations

You can build self-trust by consistently and intentionally affirming yourself—your feelings, perceptions, and choices—and by committing to treating yourself with compassion when you make a mistake. Affirmations acknowledge *your* truth or reality without judgment, so it's important to use affirmations that feel true to you.

When affirming yourself you may find these phrases helpful:

- This makes sense.

- It's okay for me to _____.

- I know what's right for me.

- This _____ [feeling/thought/choice] is valid.

- I can trust myself.

- I'm listening to my _____ [body/spirit/heart/intuition/inner wisdom].

Here are some examples:

I feel sad right now. I'm allowed to feel sad.

Not having contact with my parents makes sense for me.

I know my feelings matter. I accept and value them.

It's okay to not spend time with people who invalidate and gaslight me.

Write three or four self-validating statements of your own. Remember, they must feel true to you.

_____

_____

_____

_____

_____

Developing self-trust can be a slow process for adult children, so have patience and practice affirming yourself regularly. You can say your affirmations aloud or silently or rewrite them in your journal to reinforce these new beliefs.

How does it feel to validate yourself?

_____

Remember, growth and change often feel uncomfortable. New thoughts and behaviors usually get easier the more we practice them. So, stick with it!

Cutting Ties Can Be a Healthy Choice

Although numerous people in the US view severing family ties as wrong or bad, family scholars have begun to recognize that cutting ties with a parent can be a healthy choice for adult children who've been abused, mistreated, or rejected by their family (Agllias 2018; Allen and Moore 2017; Linden and Sillence 2021; Melvin and Hickey 2021; Scharp and Thomas 2016). We shouldn't take a one-size-fits-all approach and assume that family estrangement is always a bad choice. When individuals and communities do this, they compound adult children's pain while simultaneously stigmatizing and isolating them. I wish all families were loving, supportive, and respectful, but they aren't. The reality is that generational patterns of abuse and dysfunction are deeply entrenched in some families. Some parents lack self-awareness, don't understand or care about the harm they've caused, and refuse to learn healthy ways of relating. When we insist on maintaining family ties at any cost, we convey that the good of the whole is more important than an individual adult child's mental health and well-being. As a mental health professional, I can't get on board with this idea. Your family is *not* more important than your mental health. Your mental health matters, and prioritizing it is a healthy choice.

Here's a bit of what the literature on family estrangement tells us about the benefits of cutting ties with parents who are abusive, unsupportive, or rejecting:

- **Well-being**: 80 percent of respondents in the *Hidden Voices* survey (Stand Alone and the University of Cambridge 2015) reported that estrangement had a positive effect on their lives. They reported feeling freer, more independent, stronger, happier, less stressed, and more at peace.

- **Personal agency:** The adult children interviewed by a host of researchers (Linden and Sillence 2021; Mynard 2020; Melvin and Hickey 2021) felt empowered by their choice to reduce or cease contact with their parents. They could then make their own choices and choose the direction of their lives. They felt emotionally stronger because their parents no longer had power over them.

- **Living authentically:** Adult children noted that they were able to live more authentically after cutting ties with their families (Dorrance Hall 2018; Mynard 2020). After cutting ties, they could explore their identities, personalities, and relationships without fear of judgment or interrogation by their parents (Dorrance Hall 2018; Linden and Sillence 2021; Mynard 2020).

- **Pride:** Living authentically helps adult children develop a sense of pride in their identity (Carastathis et al. 2017; Dorrance Hall 2018; Linden and Sillence 2021; Mynard 2020). For example, some LGBTQ+ individuals who choose estrangement are no longer willing to hide their marginalized identities and instead embrace them; they derive a newfound sense of pride in being a member of the LGBTQ+ community that was not possible while maintaining a relationship with their families.

- **Optimism and hope:** Adult children who cut ties with their parents may feel greater hope and optimism about their futures. For example, some women felt more optimistic about their futures because they saw estrangement as a way to protect their children and break generational patterns of abuse (Linden and Sillence 2021).

- **Possibilities:** After cutting ties, adult children can envision more possibilities for themselves, such as career choices that their parents wouldn't approve of (Linden and Sillence 2021).

- **Resilience:** Setting boundaries, including no-contact boundaries and restricting access to personal information, can facilitate resilience among those who are marginalized or rejected by their families (Dorrance Hall 2018).

The benefits you experience may differ, of course, and it may take time for you to realize them. For now, I hope these research findings offer you hope and help challenge the assumption that family relationships are always worth preserving.

How has cutting ties been a healthy choice for you? What positive effects have you experienced thus far?

_____

_____

_____

_____

_____

Distance Makes Room for Healing

Cutting ties and feeling at peace with your decision allow healing to begin. When you were in contact with your parents or other family members who caused you harm, you probably spent a lot of time and energy worrying about, trying to avoid, defending against, and recovering from their attacks—and it's impossible to heal when you're being attacked. That's like trying to rebuild a war-torn city while bombs are still landing. This was the case for Dan. His mental health deteriorated whenever he interacted with his family, and he spent all his energy simply trying to survive. Distance gave him a reprieve and the bandwidth to develop coping skills and engage in healing activities. Like Dan, now that you've cut ties, you can focus on yourself and take steps to heal and rebuild your life. Your mind and body can relax a bit, and it's easier to take in new information and challenge negative beliefs about yourself.

You may have noticed that distance from your parents has helped you to see things more clearly. Taking a step back from a problem often gives us a new perspective; we can see more of what was going on and everyone's part in the dysfunctional family system. While you are in an abusive or dysfunctional relationship, it can be hard to see abuse or maltreatment for what it is, especially if it's the only kind of family relationship you've known. Adult children are often unsure about whether their experiences constitute verbal or emotional abuse, especially subtler forms like manipulation. It's only after they've distanced themselves that they can recognize and name abuse and feel confident that what they've experienced isn't acceptable to them and most other people.

How has distance made healing possible for you?

_____

_____

_____

_____

_____

Would healing be possible if you remained in contact with your family? Why or why not?

_____

_____

_____

_____

_____

_____

Essential Truths for Adults Who've Cut Ties with Their Parents

We all have personal rights, including the rights to be safe, to be healthy, and to feel good about ourselves. Understandably, it may be hard to believe these rights apply to you, especially if you grew up in a family in which personal rights didn't exist or had to be earned, or if institutions and legal challenges have denied your rights. Embracing your personal rights and a functional view of family estrangement is the foundation you need to love and respect yourself and feel good about your decision to cut ties.

As you read the essential truths listed here, notice how you feel; add additional truths that empower you. To reinforce these ideas, I encourage you to read this list periodically. It's also in the appendix for easy reference.

- I am a good person even if I don't have a relationship with my parents.

- It's healthy to protect and care for myself.

- It's okay to prioritize my health and happiness over family relationships.

- My family of origin is not my only or most important family. I can create a family of my choosing.

- I have a right to pursue my goals and interests and live according to my values.

- I do not need to maintain a relationship with people who are cruel or disrespectful.

- Cutting ties is an act of self-preservation, not a way to punish my family of origin.

- I deserve happiness and healing.

- I am not responsible for breaking up my family.

- My family of origin's inability to love and accept me is not a result of there being anything wrong with me. I am lovable.

- My family of origin does not determine my worth.

- I have a right to make my own choices and decide what's best for me.

- _____
- _____
- _____

Accepting Where You Are Right Now

For most adult children, cutting ties isn't a singular event; they rarely sever ties completely on the first attempt. Instead, most spend years setting boundaries and experimenting with varying amounts and types of contact before deciding what's right for them. You may have established a firm no-contact boundary, or you may still be figuring out whether you can maintain some contact. Whatever estrangement looks like for you, it's valid. The most important thing is that you establish boundaries that allow you to be a happy, healthy adult. Estrangement is a form of self-empowerment, a way of taking control and ownership of your life. So, it's important that you—not anyone else—decide how much and what type of contact to have with your family.

Establishing boundaries is a process, and pressuring yourself to decide to cut ties completely, if that's not what you need or want to do, isn't helpful for this process. Reading this book is a great way to learn about family estrangement, think about your experiences and needs, and figure out the best course of action for you. In addition, if you struggle to maintain the boundaries you've set, be kind to yourself. Being repeatedly pulled back into dysfunctional family relationships is a common pattern, not a personal failing. Families, like all systems, try to maintain the status quo, and it takes a lot of courage and energy to remove yourself from a system that you've been a part of your entire life.

Exercise: Offer Yourself Compassion

Contrary to popular belief, self-criticism doesn't motivate people to learn and change, but self-compassion can (Breines and Chen 2012; Hope, Koestner, and Milyavskaya 2014; Miyagawa, Niiya, and Taniguchi 2020; Zhang and Chen 2016). When you notice that you're being self-critical, consider whether you're judging yourself harshly. Try to replace your critical or judgmental thoughts with kindness and acceptance. A simple way to do this is to treat yourself as you would a dear friend. Answer the following prompts, and then try to treat yourself as you would a friend.

If a friend was feeling uncertain about a big decision, what would you say to them?

_____

_____

If a friend returned to an abusive relationship, what would you say to them?

_____

_____

What would you say to a friend who ceased contact with their family for reasons similar to yours?

_____

_____

Did Mina's, Juan's, and Dan's reasons for cutting ties seem valid to you? What would you say to them to alleviate their feelings of guilt?

_____

_____

_____

_____

It can be especially therapeutic to pair compassionate words with physical comfort. If you're stuck in self-criticism, offer yourself kindness and acceptance while giving yourself a hug, a neck massage, or a hot drink, or while placing your hands over your heart.

Final Thoughts

Take a moment now to consider how you feel about your decision to cut ties with your parents or a different family member. If you still have doubts, that's understandable. It's common to feel certain some days, and less certain other days. Making peace with your decision happens gradually; we all get there at our own pace. Your doubts will likely decrease as you read this book and take steps to heal, build a support network, and create a fulfilling life for yourself. You're off to a great start!

CHAPTER 3

Knowing Your Feelings Are Valid

In chapters 1 and 2, you gained clarity regarding your reasons for cutting ties with your parents, and perhaps a sense of acceptance. You know that it was an act of self-preservation. It was your best option. So, why does estrangement still hurt so much? Many adult children are surprised by how deep and long-lasting their emotional pain is, and by how confusing their feelings can be. After cutting ties you may have felt some relief and a sense of freedom after years of hurt, but cutting ties doesn't fully resolve the complex and painful feelings that most adult children experience. Estrangement creates a void, and in that space old feelings about what happened to you can surface—as well as new feelings about what it means to be estranged.

It's common to have a lot of different—sometimes conflicting—feelings about family members and your relationship with them. You may feel several emotions all at once, such as sadness and anger or guilt and relief. Or you may move back and forth between different emotions (for example, feeling discouraged one day and hopeful the next). Acknowledging your emotions and knowing you aren't the only one feeling this way is integral to healing, which is why this chapter focuses on understanding the emotional impact of cutting ties. In part 2, we'll explore ways to heal some of these painful emotions.

Practice the next exercise two or three times per day to bring yourself an awareness of your feelings. This will be helpful because awareness is the first step in effective coping.

Exercise: Notice Your Feelings

Sit quietly. Take a few deep breaths. Close your eyes, if it's comfortable to do so. Turn your attention inward. After about a minute of reflection, answer the following questions. Going forward, you can answer them in your mind or record your answers in a journal or a note-taking app.

How do you feel? Remember, you can experience multiple emotions at once.

_____

_____

Rate the intensity of your feelings on a scale of 1(barely noticeable) to 10 (most intense).

_____

Sadness

You may be confused by the sadness you feel about your estrangement, given you voluntarily chose to disconnect from your parents. Some adult children miss their families; many do not, but they still feel sad about the situation, about how they were treated, or that cutting ties was the only way to protect themselves. Feeling sad doesn't mean you regret your decision or want to reconcile. It reflects the reality that estrangement involves loss that extends far beyond the loss of a relationship with your parents. You may be grieving the loss of relationships with additional family members who took your parents' side, of family traditions, or of your dream of having a supportive family.

> **Gentle Reminder:** Loss still hurts even if you choose it.

Chances are that you're not just feeling sad about being estranged from your family. You may also feel sad about all the hurt that led up to the estrangement—the hurtful words, accusations, indifference, and rejection. Most adult children endure years of harm or emotional neglect at the hands of their parents before they decide to cut ties. So, it makes sense that feelings of sadness, or of its cousins grief, hurt, hopelessness, and numbness, may persist. You may find yourself dwelling on unanswered questions, such as:

- Why don't my parents love me?

- Why didn't they choose me?

- Why didn't anyone protect me?

- Why won't they change or apologize?

- How can parents treat their children like this?

When we don't have answers, we often blame ourselves and assume that we've done something wrong, or that we're so flawed and inadequate that we're unlovable, adding to our sorrow and hopelessness.

Sadness can appear unexpectedly, triggered by a song, smell, photograph, or memory. Seeing a happy family or watching a movie about family relationships routinely leaves some adult children in tears, especially when they're newly estranged. Again, this is often more about mourning what you didn't have than about missing your actual family. It's also common to find particular days difficult, such as holidays, birthdays, and the anniversary of your estrangement. For example, Juan, who's been estranged from his mother for eight years, rarely feels sad about his estrangement anymore. But he still slips into a "mini-depression" every year around his mother's birthday. For about three days before and two days after, his mood is low. His mother is more present in his thoughts, and he feels a sense of heaviness and dread and is unusually irritable.

What thoughts or experiences activate feelings of sadness?

_____

_____

_____

_____

_____

When do you tend to feel sad? Are there particular days or times?

_____

_____

_____

_____

How does sadness feel in your body?

_____

_____

_____

_____

What do you do when you're sad? Is this helpful? Why or why not?

_____

_____

_____

_____

Anxiety

Given what you've been through, it makes sense that you may be experiencing anxiety. Anxiety involves uncontrollable worry or rumination. Some people describe it as being stuck in a thought loop in which they rehash the same thing over and over. It's not productive; it doesn't result in new insights or solutions. Instead, it usually makes people feel worse. Anxiety also includes feeling tense, on edge, or stressed out. You may notice that your neck, back, or other muscles are tense, you're irritable, or you're having trouble sleeping.

Anxiety is a result of your body's danger alert system working in overdrive. Its job is to warn you of impending danger so you can prepare for it. This alert system is why people who are experiencing anxiety fall into "what if" thinking and often catastrophize—that is, they spend a great deal of time going over worst-case scenarios; to keep themselves safe, they want to have a plan for every terrible thing that could happen.

Most adult children who cut ties with one or more parents experienced developmental trauma. This trauma, which can include things like repeated verbal abuse and rejection, overwhelmed your ability to cope with life's challenges during childhood. This type of abuse can be traumatizing at any age. However, these experiences cause more harm and are more likely to traumatize children who are still developing physically, mentally, and emotionally. Children have limited resources, skills, and life experience to help them cope with life's challenges, so they rely on parents or caregivers to keep them safe and teach them how to overcome such challenges. However, it's likely that your parents not only failed to keep you safe but were a source of danger. Home wasn't a safe haven for you; you always had to be on alert, scanning for danger. As a result, your danger alert system is always on and you feel anxious or on edge.

> **Gentle Reminder:** Developmental trauma is never the child's fault. You didn't cause it and you couldn't control what happened to you.

Distancing yourself from a parent or family member may have reduced your anxiety and helped to calm your nervous system. However, in my experience, most adult children continue to feel anxious after cutting ties. This may be because you've been on high alert for so long and haven't yet learned effective strategies for reducing your anxiety. It's also common, especially among those who don't have a strong support network, to feel anxious about the future. Having a family, even an unsupportive one, tends to give people some sense of security or of having a safety net. For example, before his estrangement, Dan knew where he'd be spending Thanksgiving, and that he could go to his sister's if he ever needed a place to stay. After cutting ties, however, such things become sources of worry and uncertainty. It's also common to have worries related to maintaining boundaries or managing your estrangement. For example, if you live in the same town as your parents, you may worry about how you'll handle running into them or them showing up at your children's school.

Anxiety can also become intertwined with grief and sadness. Adult children commonly wonder whether their estrangement will last forever or if they'll ever see their parents or other estranged family members again. Or you may find yourself wondering how your estranged family member is doing or worrying about who will feed the dog or pay the bills now that you're gone. Again, this isn't necessarily because you miss this family member or regret your decision to leave; it's more likely due to a lack of closure and to uncertainty about the future. It's common to wonder and worry about people who've been a huge part of your life—even if you know ending the relationship was necessary.

What thoughts or experiences activate worry or anxiety?

_____

_____

_____

_____

_____

When do you tend to feel anxious?

_____

_____

_____

_____

How does anxiety feel in your body?

_____

_____

_____

_____

What do you do when you're anxious? Is this helpful? Why or why not?

_____

_____

_____

_____

_____

Anger

Some adult children feel angry all the time; they don't know how to stop feeling angry. Others rarely feel angry. Regardless of how often and intensely you experience anger, it's a difficult emotion to understand and manage. Many adult children feel ashamed of or uncomfortable with their anger because anger was mismanaged in their family of origin. It manifested as rage, aggression, or violence. Anger wasn't expressed respectfully and productively, so it feels scary, unpredictable, and confusing. Or your parents may have shown you that expressing your anger was futile—no one cared about your feelings, or you were punished for being angry. Early experiences with mismanaged anger teach children that anger is wrong, bad, scary, or selfish, making it difficult for us to acknowledge and manage our anger in adulthood.

Gentle Reminder: Feelings aren't good or bad. They help us understand ourselves and what we need.

You have a lot to be angry about, and it's okay to feel angry. It's a healthy and expected response to being mistreated or not having your needs met. Anger lets us know that something's wrong, which is why it's important to let ourselves feel angry and learn how to express anger in ways that don't harm ourselves or others. The following list may contain experiences that you feel angry about. Place a checkmark next to those that you relate to, and write in any experiences of yours that are missing.

I feel angry because…

☐ I was abused, mistreated, rejected, ignored, or unloved.

☐ My parents didn't protect me from abuse or harm.

☐ I was treated like a child even though I'm grown.

☐ My parents didn't listen to or respect me.

☐ My parents don't accept me as I am.

☐ My family conspired against me.

☐ I was the family scapegoat.

☐ I was dealt a lousy hand; my life has been harder than most people's.

☐ I had to cut ties with my family to protect myself.

☐ My parents refuse to apologize, change, or attend therapy.

☐ My friends don't understand why I'm estranged. They aren't supportive.

☐ Other people have supportive, loving families and I don't.

☐ I don't have a family. I'm all alone.

☐ _____

☐ _____

You may notice that you feel both angry and sad about these listed experiences, which makes sense because anger and sadness are closely related. They both stem from loss or hurt. Western society tends to view sadness and crying as weak. You may have been punished or chided for crying as a child, told to toughen up, or "act like a man." Such messaging can make it hard for you to access feelings of sadness and cause you to experience loss and hurt as anger rather than sadness. Or you may experience anger as sadness because anger was scary or not allowed in your family.

You may also feel angry with yourself. It's common for adult children to blame themselves for their family's problems, or for being abused. You may regret not standing up for yourself, not cutting ties sooner, or exposing your child or partner to your parents' abuse.

It's often easier for adult children to blame ourselves than to hold our parents accountable. Self-blame is the result of a dysfunctional family system that taught you that you're the cause of family conflicts, that you're bad and unlovable and deserve to be mistreated. Recognizing these beliefs as falsehoods and manipulations used to control you paves the way for healing and learning new, more accurate ways of thinking about yourself and your family.

What did you learn about anger as a child? Who was allowed to be angry? How was anger expressed? Was it useful or hurtful?

_____

_____

_____

_____

_____

What thoughts or experiences activate feelings of anger?

_____

_____

_____

_____

_____

When do you tend to feel angry?

_____

_____

_____

_____

How does anger feel in your body?

_____

_____

_____

_____

What do you do when you're angry? Is this helpful? Why or why not?

_____

_____

_____

_____

Guilt and Shame

Guilt, the feeling that you've *done* something bad or wrong, and shame, the feeling that you *are* bad or worthless, go hand in hand and often plague adult children who've cut ties with a family member. Family estrangement—regardless of its cause—is not socially acceptable in most communities, and people experiencing family estrangement tend to be judged harshly. To understand Americans' attitudes and behavior toward adults who are estranged from their parents, researchers surveyed 151 adults (Rittenour et al. 2018). The majority described such adult children as childish, immature, stubborn, selfish, ungrateful, and arrogant, reflecting a general belief that cutting ties with family members is wrong and people who do so are bad. Pervasive judgments and negative stereotypes such as these may contribute to your feelings of guilt and shame.

> **Gentle Reminder:** Other people don't get to decide what's right for you. Their disapproval doesn't make you or your choices wrong.

Feelings of guilt and shame can show up as thoughts such as:

- I'm a bad son or daughter.

- I should have tried harder to make the relationship work.

- Maybe I overreacted and it wasn't that bad.

- Everyone's family is messed up. I should've tolerated mine.

- I'm a terrible person.

- I'm unlovable.

- I'm being selfish.

- What's wrong with me?

- I screw up all my relationships.

- Maybe my parents were right and I'm the problem.

Growing up in a dysfunctional family made you susceptible to guilt and shame. Dysfunctional families use guilt and shame to control people and blame children for things they didn't cause and couldn't control. Adults who are unwilling to accept responsibility for their own mistakes and poor choices look for scapegoats—and children make perfect scapegoats because they can't stand up for themselves. Take Mina, for example. When she was young, she thought she caused her father's rage. According to him he yelled because she did things like leave her toys out. She took him at his word, not knowing that adults are responsible for managing their emotions no matter what their children do. As an adult, she knew that she wasn't responsible for her father's actions, but she couldn't shake feeling guilty and ashamed. Years of blame-shifting and scapegoating had convinced her that she was a bad daughter—messy, stupid, irresponsible, worthless—and she deserved his rage. If your family of origin led you to believe that there's something fundamentally wrong with you, you are primed to believe you are the problem, blame yourself, and second-guess your decision.

But it's not just parents who can make you feel guilty. Even friends and loved ones such as life partners can send the message that cutting ties with your parents is wrong. Folks I know who are estranged from a parent frequently hear judgmental comments and questions like the ones listed below. Perhaps you've heard something similar from friends or family members. You can note those specific to your situation on the blank lines.

- Give them another chance. You only get one family.

- They're your parents, don't you miss them?

- You'll regret it if they die and you never said goodbye or reconciled.

- You should forgive them.

- They did the best they could.

- How can you abandon your parents after all they've done for you?

- Scripture says you should honor and obey your parents.

- You're being selfish.

- They don't deserve this.

- You can't keep a grandmother from her grandchild. That's just cruel!

- It's unhealthy to hold a grudge.

- _____

- _____

Messages like these are not only painful, they invalidate your feelings and experiences and imply or overtly state that you're a bad person and you've done something wrong. They contribute to feelings of guilt and shame, which make it hard to see cutting ties as a healthy choice and to move forward. Keep in mind that judgment and criticism can also be subtle—a sideways glance, a heavy sigh, or an eye roll, for example. Not all judgment is verbal.

It's hard not to internalize criticism and judgment, especially that coming from loved ones, friends, and people who are skilled at using guilt and shame to manipulate you. As you move through the healing process, you'll learn how to challenge feelings of guilt and shame, recognize your self-worth, and set boundaries with people who try to make you feel bad about yourself and your choices.

What thoughts or experiences activate feelings of guilt or shame?

_____

_____

_____

_____

_____

When do you tend to feel guilty or ashamed?

_____

_____

_____

_____

How do guilt and shame feel in your body?

_____

_____

_____

_____

What do you do when you feel guilty or ashamed? Is this helpful? Why or why not?

_____

_____

_____

_____

Loneliness

Emotional pain is often reduced when we share it with people who understand; we feel less alone and ashamed when we know we're not the only ones feeling this way or struggling with family problems. Unfortunately, friends and family members don't always provide the support, compassion, and understanding that adult children need, making estrangement a lonely experience.

Gentle Reminder: You aren't alone; others can relate to your experiences and feelings, even if you haven't met them yet.

Sometimes, friends and family don't offer support because they don't know how or don't realize that you need it. People who've never experienced family estrangement tend to misunderstand the experience. As a result, they may unknowingly minimize your pain or wrongly assume that it's "just a phase" or that a single argument got out of hand. They may see the estrangement as a finite event and wonder why you aren't "over it" already. They don't recognize how much you've lost and how painful it is to cut ties with your parents, so they don't go out of their way to be supportive.

It's also possible that your friends and acquaintances don't offer support because they don't know what you're going through. Research has shown that adult children are reluctant to talk about their estrangement because they fear being judged or dismissed (Agllias 2018; Blake 2017; Rittenour et al. 2018; Scharp 2016). This makes sense given the social stigma attached to estrangement and lack of understanding coming from friends and family. All it takes is a few judgmental or insensitive comments from their social network to cause most people to clam up. When we're hurting and others haven't shown up for us in the ways we need, it's often safer to suffer in silence than to reach out for support and risk being hurt or disappointed yet again.

You may also avoid telling people you're estranged because you don't want to burden them. For example, you might wish your neighbor would invite you to her holiday party—and you know she would if she knew you were alone—but you worry that you'd spoil her family time or be an imposition. So, you avoid talking about the holidays altogether and spend them alone. The discomfort that's felt from talking about estrangement can go both ways. Friends, colleagues, and neighbors who know about your estrangement may also avoid talking to you about it or exclude you from events that they think might make you sad (Rittenour et al. 2018). Having friends and family ignore your feelings or exclude you from events can lead to an increase in feelings of sadness, anxiety, anger, guilt, and shame.

Estrangement is also lonely because cutting ties with one family member can negatively impact other relationships (Scharp 2016). Sometimes, people don't know how to navigate the challenges of having a relationship with family members who are estranged from each other and find it easier to pick a side than to be stuck in the middle of a family conflict. All too often, family members side with the aggressor and choose team mom and dad. Countless adult children have told me about a parent bad-mouthing them to the rest of the family, spreading lies, or otherwise manipulating family members into turning against them. Sometimes this behavior reaches beyond the extended family, and an entire community abandons an adult child who cut ties with their parents. This can cause a profound sense of loneliness.

Perhaps you've also chosen to end relationships with unsupportive friends, siblings, or extended family members, especially if they won't stop pressuring you to reconcile with your parents (Scharp 2016). This was true for Mina. After she cut ties with her father, her mother continuously pressured her to forgive her father— and this damaged the relationship between Mina and her mother. In my therapy practice, I've witnessed how devastating and manipulative the pressure to reconcile can be. Some adult children find it so painful that they give in to the pressure and resume contact with their parents. This is understandable given the intensity of the pressure and our need for human connection and belonging. Typically, the reconciliation is short-lived because nothing of consequence has changed in the relationship. For some, the only way to cope with coercion and guilt trips is to cease or limit contact with those pushing them to reconcile. In the wake of your estrangement, you may find your support system dwindling because so few people understand why you cut ties, see it as a healthy choice, or are willing to sit with you in your sadness, anxiety, anger, and shame.

How has estrangement from your parents negatively impacted other relationships?

_____

_____

_____

_____

_____

What thoughts or experiences activate feelings of loneliness?

_____

_____

_____

_____

When do you tend to feel lonely?

_____

_____

_____

_____

How does loneliness feel in your body?

_____

_____

_____

_____

What do you do when you feel lonely? Is this helpful? Why or why not?

_____

_____

_____

_____

Final Thoughts

The pain of family estrangement is real. You aren't hurting because you've done something wrong or you're a bad person. You aren't overreacting and you aren't being too sensitive. Estrangement is a deep wound—as are the experiences that led up to it. However, painful experiences can lead to personal growth when we consistently do the work needed to heal ourselves. When you're ready, chapter 4 will help you get started!

Part 2

Healing

CHAPTER 4

Grieving Your Losses

Grieving is hard, which is why so many people try to avoid it. It's also complicated when it's a loss that you chose and so many misunderstand. You might be tempted to skip this chapter, either because grieving feels overwhelming or because you don't think you need to grieve. However, I encourage you to read this chapter with an open mind, try the exercises, and consider how fully acknowledging your losses and allowing yourself to grieve might help you feel stronger, more in control, and freer.

What Is Grief?

Grief is a natural and automatic response to loss. When you experience a loss, your body, mind, and spirit feel it even if you don't consciously acknowledge it. The question isn't *whether* you'll respond to a loss, but *how*.

Grief manifests in many ways; it can affect your emotions, physical health, and thoughts. It's common to have a variety of symptoms and for them to vary day by day or even hour by hour. For example, you might feel hopeless and tearful one day and feel angry and have a terrible headache the next.

What does your grief feel like? Note the grief-related emotions, thoughts, and physical symptoms you've had.

_____

_____

_____

_____

_____

Why You Need to Grieve

Doing things to grieve or actively acknowledge our emotions and losses helps us work through them and move forward with our lives. If you ignore emotions, such as sadness and anger, you can get stuck in them. Or you may engage in unhealthy coping strategies—like drinking too much or numbing out with food, TV, or gaming. Ignoring or numbing our pain doesn't typically work in the long term. Our feelings of loss will keep showing up until we acknowledge and deal with them, making it hard for us to feel in control of our emotions and lives.

That's why it's important to engage in *grief work*—the active and intentional process of accepting and coping with your losses.

> **Gentle Reminder:** You need to grieve, even if you're happy or relieved to be free of your parents.

What's made it hard for you to grieve?

_____

_____

_____

_____

_____

Various models and theories can help guide your grief work. However, most of them were designed for those grieving the death of a loved one. Estrangement is a different type of loss. So, before we delve into how to grieve estrangement-related losses, let's recognize the challenges this form of grieving presents.

Why Grieving Estrangement Is So Hard

Grieving an estrangement is quite different from grieving the death of a loved one. Estrangement is a unique form of loss for which the losses are not always tangible or easy to describe (Agllias 2011; 2018; Conti 2015). You may not miss your parents per se, but there's still a sense of loss related to not having a mother or father or not having the parents you longed for. For some, there's a profound sense of grief that comes with acknowledging that they're never going to have a functional relationship with their parents, that their parents aren't going to change, and that their parents aren't ever going to be the parents they need them to be.

Most adult children experience numerous losses beyond the loss of connection with a parent. Let's look at Mina's and Dan's experiences as examples.

• *Mina*

Mina, who cut ties with her domineering parents, feels incredibly hurt and sad about the way things ended with her parents. However, she doesn't miss them. For the most part, she's relieved to be free of them and their constant criticism and invalidation. She does, however, miss having a connection to her family history and culture. She misses her mother's cooking and wishes she had the family recipes that only her mother knows. She lost access to family photos, including those from her childhood. And although Mina knows it's best that her daughter doesn't have a relationship with her parents, she's sad that her daughter will never have the quintessential grandparent experiences—baking cookies, going fishing, or reading together—nor learn family traditions from them.

- ## *Dan*

Unlike Mina, Dan misses his parents, sister, and extended family. When he was a young child they had good times together, and he has happy memories of vacations, Christmases, and family reunions. He misses having a family to spend the holidays with. As a young man, he misses the practical support that most of his peers get from their parents. He fumbled through doing his taxes and buying a used car without any guidance. In both cases he felt certain he'd done something wrong that would lead to financial ruin and wished he'd had a parent to turn to.

Gentle Reminder: You can miss someone and not want them back in your life.

What stood out to you about Mina's and Dan's losses?

_____

_____

_____

_____

What about their losses makes it hard for them to grieve?

_____

_____

_____

_____

Ambiguous Loss and Disenfranchised Grief

The concepts of ambiguous loss and disenfranchised grief can help us understand the complex form of grief that results from estrangement. Psychologist Pauline Boss (2006) coined the term "ambiguous loss" to explain the challenges people face when grieving the loss of someone who is gone but not necessarily deceased, as is the case when a loved one is "lost" to addiction or dementia, has been kidnapped, is placed for adoption, or is estranged.

An ambiguous loss is believed to be more stressful than other losses because there is no closure or certainty about whether the "missing" person will return or the relationship will be restored. In the case of estrangement, this includes the confusing contradiction of simultaneously having a parent and not having a parent. For example, if you're estranged from your mother, you technically have a mother, but you don't have a mother in the practical sense because you don't have a relationship with her, you never see her, you don't know what's happening in her life, and she doesn't do motherly things for you. An ambiguous loss also leaves you uncertain. It's unclear what will happen to the relationship; you might remain estranged forever or you might not. You don't know for sure, and the lack of finality makes it difficult to grieve.

Disenfranchised grief is the result of a loss that is stigmatized or not socially acknowledged, such as a loved one being incarcerated or the loss related to an abortion (Doka 1989). Estrangement also creates disenfranchised grief because many cultures misunderstand and fail to recognize the losses attached to it. For example, there's no bereavement leave after you've cut ties with your parents. There are relatively few supportive resources for people experiencing estrangement compared to the resources available for individuals grieving a death. People may not even realize you're grieving because there's no public announcement, event, or ritual to mark the end of a relationship. And you may feel ashamed of your family circumstances, so you don't ask for support.

All cultures have rituals or customs that help grievers cope when a loved one has died. For example, mourners may attend a funeral mass, sit shiva, create a Día de los Muertos altar, and eat—or not eat—particular foods. Take a moment to think about what's typically done in your family, culture, or community to say goodbye or mark the end of someone's life. How do friends and family members typically support someone when a family member has died? In some cultures, people send flowers or bring casseroles. Or they might pray or sit with you. However, when your loss is due to estrangement, most of these grieving rituals don't apply. There's usually no acknowledgment of your loss. People don't show support and help you through your grief as they might if your parent had died. Adult children who are estranged are often alone in their grief—and that makes it more painful.

What, if any, support and comfort did you receive from others in relation to your estrangement?

_____

_____

_____

_____

> **Gentle Reminder:** Not receiving support is another loss that many adult children who are estranged experience.

Previous Losses

Estrangement may also reactivate or remind you of other painful losses. For example, as Juan grieved his estrangement, he started thinking more about his biological father, whom he never knew, and the typical childhood experiences and opportunities he missed out on because he had to grow up too fast. You may not be consciously aware of which losses are resurfacing as they may be losses that you haven't specifically grieved but are significant nonetheless. We often underestimate the impact of nondeath losses, like those related to divorce, miscarriage, job loss, illness, natural disasters, social injustice, or the COVID-19 pandemic. If we don't acknowledge and grieve our losses, they tend to pile up, making new losses feel even heavier and more complex. Even a minor loss, like a lost phone, can trigger a strong reaction that feels disproportionate because it stirs up past losses.

What previous losses have been on your mind recently?

_____

_____

_____

_____

_____

Are there other previous losses that might be unconsciously resurfacing as you grieve the end of your relationship with your parents?

_____

_____

_____

_____

_____

When you're experiencing strong emotions, remember that your grief is likely compounded by previous losses, both big and small, and your feelings are valid. Recognizing this can help you be patient and kind with yourself during the grieving process, rather than minimizing your pain.

Write a brief note of comfort to yourself to help you through this difficult time.

_____

_____

_____

_____

_____

How to Grieve Estrangement Losses

Grieving is a personal experience, and there's no right or wrong way to do it. What you find helpful may depend on your personality and preferences, lived experiences, health, spiritual beliefs, cultural heritage, family traditions, and where you are in the grief process. This section will guide you through three tasks of grieving:

1. Acknowledge and validate your losses.

2. Process your feelings.

3. Comfort yourself.

In future chapters, we'll address two additional tasks of grieving—building a support network and engaging in meaningful, joyful activities after loss. These tasks are derived from ambiguous loss theory (Boss 1999; 2006), disenfranchised grief theory (Doka 1989), and Worden's (2009) framework for mourning. Keep in mind that we don't necessarily work through these tasks in order or one at a time. They're ongoing processes that you'll work on concurrently and revisit multiple times.

Acknowledge and Validate Your Losses

Acknowledging your losses is a good place to begin your grief work because you need to know what you're grieving. As I mentioned earlier, your losses may not be obvious. So, you need to bring them into conscious awareness. You can do this by reading the list that follows and checking the losses you relate to. You may feel some of these losses strongly and others not at all—and that may change over time. For example, if you're a young, healthy person you might not feel any loss related to not having access to family medical history, but that may change as you age.

- ☐ Being part of a family (not necessarily *your* family, but *a* family)
- ☐ Relationships with extended family members
- ☐ Family activities, such as holidays, reunions, or Sunday dinners
- ☐ Cultural knowledge, traditions, recipes, stories, and practices
- ☐ Family history, stories, or photos
- ☐ Access to family medical history
- ☐ Your childhood home or hometown
- ☐ Family as a safety net
- ☐ Practical or financial support
- ☐ Opportunities

☐ Your role as a _____ (daughter, brother, grandchild, and so forth)

☐ The possibility of closure

☐ The love and support you longed for

☐ Sense of belonging

☐ Feeling safe

☐ Self-esteem or self-confidence

☐ Health and well-being

What other losses related to your estrangement have you experienced?

_____

_____

_____

_____

_____

_____

What, if anything, do you miss about your parents or family? (Remember, you can miss things and still not want them back.)

_____

_____

_____

_____

_____

_____

Gentle Reminder: You can miss something even if you never had it.

Exercise: Validate Your Losses

Validating your losses means recognizing that they are real, even if others don't acknowledge them, and that it's natural to struggle with and have feelings about them. You can validate your losses with a statement such as:

- This loss is real.

- This is an ambiguous loss.

- It's okay to grieve this loss.

- My loss is real, even if others can't see it.

Identify a specific loss you've experienced and acknowledge it with a validation statement.

Example: I've lost the possibility of closure with my father. This is an ambiguous loss and it's okay for me to grieve it.

I've lost _____ [specific loss].

Statement of validation: _____

Repeat this exercise for each loss you identify using a separate journal or the worksheet available for download at this book's website, http://www.newharbinger.com/53905, where you'll find other useful free tools.

Process Your Feelings

Processing your feelings is another central task of grief work. It involves noticing your feelings, being curious about them, exploring what they mean, and trying to accept them. As you grieve, be mindful that you aren't minimizing your feelings, suppressing them, or telling yourself that you shouldn't feel this way.

There are a variety of ways to process your feelings. I've provided some suggestions, but don't be limited by these ideas. I encourage you to be creative and experiment with different approaches. You can place a checkmark next to the ideas that appeal to you and list additional ideas in the space provided.

- ☐ Name what you're feeling. I feel sad right now because _____.

- ☐ Cry. Crying provides a physical and emotional release.

- ☐ Sit quietly. Notice what feelings emerge.

- ☐ Reflect on or write about what you've lost.

- ☐ Reflect on or write about any happy memories that you want to preserve.

- ☐ Write a poem or song.

- ☐ Make a condolence card for yourself.

☐   Write a goodbye letter. (Don't send it; this is for your processing only.)

☐   Draw, paint, or engage in other creative outlets.

☐   Listen to music. Music evokes feelings.

☐   Exercise. Movement provides a physical release for emotions and muscle tension.

☐   _____

☐   _____

☐   _____

Recall any grieving rituals or cultural practices you used when a loved one died. How might you use or adapt them to help process your estrangement losses?

_____

_____

_____

_____

_____

_____

Exercise: Journaling to Process Loss

Guided journaling can also bring awareness to your emotions and help you process them. You can use some or all of the following prompts for journaling, and repeat the process as often as is helpful. This worksheet is available for download at this book's website, http://www.newharbinger.com/53905.

What loss is weighing on your heart and mind today?

_____

_____

_____

_____

_____

When you think of this loss, how do you feel?

_____

_____

_____

_____

_____

_____

Dig a little deeper. Are there any other emotions hidden beneath the ones you noticed first?

_____

_____

_____

_____

_____

_____

Where do you feel this loss in your body? What physical sensations do you notice?

_____

_____

_____

_____

_____

_____

What does it mean to accept this loss?

_____

_____

_____

_____

_____

_____

What would it be like to let go of the pain associated with this particular loss? How might you start?

_____

_____

_____

_____

_____

_____

Processing your feelings can be a painful endeavor, and it's common to feel worse before you feel better. Your emotions may be raw and intense—and it takes time to make sense of them, accept them, and heal. During this process, it's especially important to comfort yourself.

Comfort Yourself

Grieving takes a lot out of us, physically and emotionally. Therefore, we need to give ourselves extra care and comfort. Take a moment to consider what helps you feel cared for and safe. If you're not sure, that's okay. This list offers some ideas. Place a checkmark next to those that appeal to you.

☐ Wrap yourself in a weighted blanket.

☐ Find comfort in simple, consistent routines. This could include a short daily walk, eating dinner with your partner, or cleaning the kitchen.

☐ Spend time outside. Nature has a restorative, soothing quality.

☐ Spend time with your pets. Pets provide unconditional love that can be healing and calming.

☐ Treat yourself to a calming self-care ritual, such as a hot bath, massage, or mindful coffee break.

☐ Light a candle.

☐ Pray.

☐ Meditate.

☐ Plant a garden, flowers, or a tree.

☐ Buy yourself a small gift.

☐ Get extra rest.

☐ Visit a favorite place.

☐ Say something kind or encouraging to yourself, such as "This is tough, and I'll get through it."

You can also identify comforting practices by tuning in to your preferences. Note your favorite things below so you can incorporate them into your self-comfort activities.

Favorite ways to relax:

_____

_____

Favorite edible treats:

_____

_____

Favorite nonfood treats:

_____

_____

Favorite movies, TV shows, games, books, or music:

_____

_____

Places where you feel safe, relaxed, or at peace:

_____

_____

People or animals that can provide comfort:

_____

_____

Using what you know about yourself, identify several additional comforting activities.

_____

_____

_____

_____

_____

Make Time for Grieving

Some find it helpful, especially in the beginning, to schedule time for grief work daily or weekly. This ensures that they prioritize their feelings and needs.

When will you grieve? I encourage you to look at your calendar and block off time for intentional grief work. This might include the time you'll spend reading this book, seeing your therapist, and engaging in the activities discussed in this chapter.

_____

_____

_____

_____

If you don't proactively spend time grieving, you'll likely experience more of the grief-related symptoms discussed at the beginning of this chapter. Or your grief may show up at inopportune times, such as crying during a business meeting.

How will you know that you need to dedicate more time to grief work? What physical symptoms, emotions, or behaviors might be cues?

_____

_____

_____

_____

_____

Final Thoughts

Grieving is a complicated process, and although it can be exhausting, lengthy, and marked by ups and downs, you're off to a good start. Your losses are real and deserve to be acknowledged and grieved. So, try not to push your grief away, minimize your pain, or set timelines for when you should be done grieving. By making time and space for your grief, and by offering yourself comfort and compassion, you're taking steps to heal. If you keep at it, I'm confident that you'll see progress.

CHAPTER 5

Releasing Anger and Shame

In this chapter, we're going to focus on two uncomfortable emotions: anger and shame. Like grief, they're normal responses to loss. Many of us aren't sure how to manage anger and shame, so we try to avoid them. They also tend to be deeply entrenched, meaning they have a strong hold on us. They may even be central to how you see yourself. You may think of yourself as an "angry person" or a "worthless person." When we overidentify with a feeling and let it define us, it's harder to change or let go of it. But change is possible! So, let's spend some time understanding these emotions, where they come from, how they impact us, and how to release them.

Anger

First, I want to reiterate that there is nothing wrong with feeling angry. Anger serves a purpose, often to let us know when something is wrong. Anger is a natural, protective response to being mistreated, not getting what we need, and not being listened to or understood. Anger alerts you to danger and can propel you into action. For example, it can be the impetus for ending an abusive relationship and help you make choices going forward that are in your best interest.

Sometimes we equate anger with violence, but this is inaccurate. Anger is an emotion, not an action. Violence is harmful, destructive behavior that often stems from feeling angry. Anger can be expressed in many ways, and it isn't always as a destructive force. That being said, anger can be problematic if it keeps us stuck in the past or results in us harming ourselves or others. For example, anger can contribute to depression, negative self-talk, and self-sabotage, such as procrastinating, binge drinking, or isolating. We can harm others and relationships when we take our anger out on them by yelling, being physically aggressive, or blaming them, for example. Anger can consume us, making it hard to imagine things working out for us and closing us off from new relationships and opportunities.

Take a moment to reflect on how your anger has been both helpful and unhelpful.

How has feeling angry helped you? For example, has it alerted you to danger or helped you protect yourself?

_____

_____

_____

How has anger been a problem for you?

_____

_____

_____

_____

What would a healthy relationship with anger look like for you?

_____

_____

_____

_____

Because anger gives us valuable information, we don't want to ignore it, and never being angry shouldn't be our goal. We need to allow ourselves to feel angry, be curious about what it means, notice signs of anger, and have healthy ways to release it.

Give Yourself Permission to Feel Angry

Letting yourself feel angry can be scary, even when you know anger serves a purpose. A lot of us were taught that anger is bad or dangerous—and that good people don't feel angry. And many of us have been harmed by other people's mismanaged anger. Suppressing our anger is understandable but not helpful. Anger doesn't go away just because we try to ignore it. Imagine yourself as a cup with a finite amount of space to hold your anger. When it's full, your anger will spill out and make a mess—you'll lash out, do things you regret, or feel out of control. And holding in all that anger can contribute to stress-related health problems.

It's more productive to permit yourself to feel angry. The process of acknowledging your feelings and accepting them without judgment can help you better understand yourself and what you need. And when you recognize that your emotions are painful, you can offer yourself compassion. The next exercise will help you get started. If anger is an uncomfortable emotion for you, you'll want to repeat the exercise regularly. You can download a copy of it at this book's website, http://www.newharbinger.com/53905, where you'll also find other useful free tools.

Exercise: Allow Yourself to Feel Angry

With a specific person or situation in mind, write about what created feelings of anger.

_____

_____

_____

_____

_____

Write a self-validating statement about your anger.

Example: *Anyone who's experienced what I've been through would be angry.*

_____

In addition to anger, what other emotions did you have about this person or situation?

_____

_____

_____

What did you need or want in this situation?

_____

_____

_____

How can you give yourself comfort or kindness?

_____

_____

_____

Post-exercise reflection: What was it like to acknowledge and accept feelings of anger?

_____

_____

_____

Notice Signs of Anger

Anger is easy to spot when we're yelling or cursing, but we often miss the more subtle signs of anger or cues indicating the intensity of our anger is increasing. If we can notice and address feelings of anger as they occur and use healthy strategies to reduce existing anger, we can avoid having our anger spill out and doing things that are dangerous or harmful. Early signs of anger can be physical sensations, such as your heart racing, tingling in your extremities, sweating, or fatigue. They can also be thoughts, such as *I hate her* or *I can't do this anymore*. You might fixate on a person or event that contributed to your anger. Also, pay attention to behaviors like pacing, avoidance, clenching your fists or jaw, eating junk food, or smoking, which may reflect feelings of anger or frustration.

What are early warning signs that you're getting angry?

_____

_____

_____

_____

_____

There may also be external events that routinely create feelings of anger, such as someone cutting you off in traffic or your coworker ignoring you. Being aware of events that trigger your anger can also help you recognize that your anger is building.

What are some external situations or events that trigger anger for you?

_____

_____

_____

Exercise: Anger Awareness

Tracking is an easy and effective way to increase awareness of anything you want to change. Make an entry on the chart whenever you notice even a low level of anger. Alternatively, if you rarely feel angry, intentionally check in with yourself and make an entry twice per day to practice noticing your emotions. You can download this chart at this book's website, http://www.newharbinger.com/53905.

Date	Rate the intensity of your anger on a scale from 1 (barely noticeable) to 10 (most intense anger ever).	Choose a word to describe how you feel (e.g., pissed, upset, mad, irate).	Briefly describe the situation or anger trigger.	Note your bodily sensations (e.g., a pit in your stomach, racing heart).

What did you learn by tracking your anger? Did you identify any patterns, early signs, or triggers?

_____

_____

_____

_____

When your anger level is 5 or higher, or it's rising day after day, you should take steps to release it in a healthy manner. Let's turn our attention to how to accomplish this.

Ways to Manage or Release Anger

We all need ways to process and release feelings of anger. You may find a combination of strategies helpful as they each offer something different. Use the following list to help you generate ideas, which you can write in at the end of the list. Then, answer the questions that follow and try the next exercise.

- Physical activity helps us metabolize stress hormones and release muscle tension. In addition to following a regular exercise routine, when you notice anger building do something physical, such as dancing, jumping jacks, walking, or kicking a soccer ball for a few minutes.

- Write or talk about your feelings with a trusted friend or therapist.

- Prioritize relaxing activities whether it's knitting, reading for pleasure, or sitting in the sunshine.

- Use mindfulness practices to bring awareness to your feelings and help you accept and tolerate them. These include meditation, breathing exercises, naming your feelings, and reminding yourself that your feelings are valid.

- Take a time-out from a stressful or upsetting conversation or situation to clear your head and regroup. During your time-out, try one of the other suggested activities (a short walk or breathing exercise, for example.)

- Get enough sleep. When you're tired, you're more likely to be irritable and lose your temper.

- Avoid alcohol and other mood-altering substances that can increase reactivity.

- _____

- _____

What strategies will you try?

_____

_____

How will you know if they're effective?

_____

_____

Exercise: Accept Anger Without Overidentifying with It

This simple mindfulness exercise can help you accept your emotions in the moment without overidentifying with them, because doing so can prevent you from experiencing other emotions and seeing the world more objectively. Repeat this mantra to yourself or write it in a journal any time you notice feelings of anger. Please note that you can use this mantra for *any* emotion that makes you uncomfortable, not just anger.

I notice that I feel angry.

My anger does not define me. I am not my thoughts and emotions.

Everyone feels angry at times. I accept my feelings and choose to be gentle with myself.

Use this space to rewrite the mantra, making any changes you find helpful.

_____

_____

_____

_____

Forgiveness Is Optional

Many adult children wrestle with whether to forgive their parents or others who have harmed them. For some, forgiveness is a helpful endeavor that facilitates them to let go of their anger and resentment and make peace with what happened. However, for others forgiveness feels like letting the perpetrators off the hook, that what they did is over and done with and they are absolved. Being told to forgive adds insult to injury when you're still dealing with the aftermath of the abuse you experienced and the perpetrator's wrongs have not been made right. It's especially hard to forgive someone if they haven't acknowledged the harm they caused, apologized, and made amends, which is typical in cases of estrangement. So, while forgiveness is something that one usually does for oneself, not for the perpetrator, it's still a notion that many understandably reject.

Forgiveness is a personal decision. It isn't right or wrong. Forgiving isn't morally superior, and it's not essential to your healing. Pressuring yourself to forgive will probably make you feel worse, not better. As I said earlier, anger is an appropriate response to being mistreated. Certainly, you don't want your anger to prevent you from living the life you want, but you also don't need to quickly push it aside because you've been told that forgiveness is the "right" thing to do. What matters most is that you make the decision to do what is best for you.

> **Gentle Reminder:** Healing is not contingent on you forgiving your parents.

If it seems like forgiveness might be helpful for you in moving forward, you can explore it and work toward it. If you're not sure, you can revisit it at another time. Or, if it's a distasteful idea, you can use the other strategies in this book to gradually let go of the anger that's getting in your way. Take a few minutes now to explore your thoughts and feelings about forgiveness.

What does forgiveness mean to you?

_____

_____

How do you feel about forgiving your parents or family? What do you think that feeling is telling you?

_____

_____

_____

Is forgiveness a goal? Why or why not?

_____

_____

_____

If you want to forgive, how might you start the process?

_____

_____

If not, how can you keep anger from ruling your life?

_____

_____

Although forgiveness does not need to be part of your healing process, it's crucial for you to know and wholeheartedly believe that your family's inability to love and respect you isn't the result of you being defective or difficult. It's a result of their deficiencies and problems. I've noticed that distance helps my clients see their family dysfunction more clearly. After cutting ties, the ways they were abused or mistreated are clearer, and they can situate their experiences in a generational pattern of abuse, substance misuse, mental illness, or other trauma or dysfunction. As a result, they recognize that their parents or other family members have limitations and problems that have nothing to do with them—and, whether they forgive or not, this recognition can help them release some of the anger they feel toward their perpetrators and focus on building a safe and satisfying life separate from their family of origin.

Let Go of Self-Directed Anger

It's also common to be angry with yourself for investing so much time and energy into trying to fix your relationship with your parents or for allowing yourself to be mistreated. Children are scapegoated and harshly criticized in dysfunctional families. Over time they internalize their parents' critical voices and become excessively hard on themselves.

When you notice self-critical thoughts, try to respond with self-compassion and acceptance rather than self-contempt. Acting as the loving parent you never had breaks the cycle of internalized abuse. Here are a few phrases you can try saying to yourself or aloud:

- I'm allowed to make mistakes and change my mind. I don't need to be perfect.

- I choose to forgive myself for the mistakes I've made.

- I would do things differently now, but I did the best I could at the time.

- Dwelling on the past and beating myself up isn't helpful. Instead, I will stay focused on the present and use what I have learned.

- Using all that I've learned I will not judge my past behavior.

Which ones resonate with you? You can also write your own.

_____

_____

Feeling worthy and lovable is a big undertaking for most adult children who've cut ties with a family member. In the next section, we're going to talk more about how to rid yourself of shame and increase your sense of self-worth.

Shame

Shame is painful. Feeling shame reflects a core belief that you're defective and unlovable. It's more than thinking you've *done* something bad or wrong. Shame defines who you are. It tells you that you *are* inherently flawed or worthless, which is why shame persists no matter how much you accomplish nor how perfect or altruistic you are. Feeling worthless takes a toll on your mental health, making it hard to establish healthy relationships, pursue your goals, practice self-care, and set boundaries.

Shame is a common feeling among adult children who are estranged from their parents. Which of these signs of shame do you identify with?

- ☐ You feel worthless.

- ☐ You feel like a burden.

- ☐ You think you have nothing of value to contribute.

- ☐ You think you ruin everything.

- ☐ Sometimes you wish you'd never been born.

- ☐ You expect everyone will abandon or reject you.

- ☐ You feel like a failure.

- ☐ You think everything's your fault.

- ☐ You don't trust compliments or praise.

- ☐ You're conflict avoidant or a people pleaser.

- ☐ You act like a chameleon, morphing into who people want you to be.

- ☐ You set impossibly high standards for yourself.

- ☐ You compare yourself to others and feel inadequate.

- ☐ You're afraid of failure.
- ☐ You work excessively.
- ☐ You struggle to identify anything good about yourself.
- ☐ You have all-or-nothing thinking.
- ☐ You worry about what others think of you.
- ☐ You feel like you don't belong anywhere.
- ☐ You apologize when you haven't done anything wrong.

How has shame affected you? For example, has it impacted your career path or work performance, relationships, health, and so forth?

_____

_____

_____

_____

_____

_____

Shame is a heavy load to bear, and unfortunately there's no quick fix for it. However, by understanding where these feelings and beliefs came from, you can chart a path to healing.

> **Gentle Reminder:** Self-absorbed, immature, and insecure adults shame and criticize others to make themselves appear superior. This is abusive behavior, especially when an adult does it to a child.

Exercise: Explore the Roots of Shame

Family estrangement can be a source of shame. In addition, you likely internalized feelings of worthlessness, inadequacy, and unlovability long before you severed ties with your family or a single family member. In this exercise, you're going to explore how your childhood experiences contributed to the shame you feel today. It's emotionally taxing work. So, if you don't have the bandwidth to do it now, come back to it when you feel stronger. Take your time with these questions and be gentle with yourself. This is hard but important work! If you have a therapist, you may want to check in with them for added support along the way.

For each question, write about the experience and how it led to feelings of shame. Before you begin, place both hands over your heart as a self-loving gesture and feel your body breathing. Take several slow, deep breaths. Anytime you feel overwhelmed, anxious, or like you're shutting down during this exercise, pause and place your hands over your heart to center yourself.

How did your parents respond when you made mistakes? How did this affect your sense of self-worth?

_____

_____

_____

_____

_____

Did your parents recognize or encourage your strengths, talents, and goals? If they didn't, how did that impact you?

_____

_____

_____

_____

_____

Were you allowed or encouraged to be your authentic self? If not, how did that impact you?

_____

_____

_____

_____

_____

Were you allowed or encouraged to have your own beliefs and ideas and make your own choices? If not, how did that impact you?

_____

_____

_____

_____

_____

What memories do you have of being shamed or humiliated as a child? How did those experiences affect you?

_____

_____

_____

_____

_____

Were you blamed for your parents' problems, such as substance use or mental health issues, or expected to keep family secrets? If so, how has that impacted you?

_____

_____

_____

_____

_____

How did other childhood experiences contribute to you feeling worthless, inadequate, unlovable, or defective?

_____

_____

_____

_____

_____

Thinking about how your family has harmed you can be heartbreaking, infuriating, and overwhelming. Take a moment now to check in with yourself.

How do you feel? What do you need?

_____

_____

_____

_____

You've expended a lot of emotional energy during this exercise; it might feel good to take a break and do something restorative, such as calling a friend, saying something kind to yourself, or even crying.

What would feel restorative to you?

_____

_____

Change False Narratives

When you've been steeped in shame for your entire life, it's hard to accept that much of what you were taught about yourself is wrong. For example, it's much easier for me to see my clients' good qualities, talents, and strengths, and the ways they enrich their communities, than it is for them. That's because living with shame is like being surrounded by fun house mirrors: you only see a skewed and inaccurate version of yourself, one that you learned in childhood. Recovering from internalized shame is a big undertaking. It involves questioning your beliefs about yourself and reconstructing them with a foundation of healthy self-esteem. To start, try out the idea that you are good enough. You don't have to completely believe it, just consider the possibility—and know that you can choose what you think and feel about yourself.

What does it feel like to consider that you're a good and worthwhile person—even if you can't see it?

_____

_____

_____

_____

The next exercise will help you examine your beliefs about yourself more systematically and decide if they're accurate and helpful. Before starting the exercise, consider these common negative core beliefs of adult children who are estranged from their parents or other family members. I am:

- Unlovable
- Unwanted
- Difficult
- Needy
- Stupid
- Incompetent

- Selfish
- Damaged
- A mistake
- Ugly
- Worthless
- A failure

Exercise: Change Negative Beliefs About Yourself

1. **Identify a negative core belief you have about yourself.** This is a strong belief that defines who you are. Example: *I'm needy.*

    _____

2. **Where did you learn this belief?** Core beliefs usually stem from childhood experiences. Example: *My mother frequently told me I was needy and ignored me. My father yelled at me for crying.*

    _____

    _____

    _____

    _____

3. **Consider other perspectives.** Challenge your belief by considering alternate perspectives and explanations. For example, instead of assuming that your parents are correct in their assessment of your neediness, identify other *possible* ways to understand yourself and your behavior. Example: *I cried frequently because I was ignored and yelled at.*

    _____

    _____

    _____

    _____

4. **Reframe your belief.** Recognizing that there are many alternative ways to understand yourself and your behavior, choose to view yourself in a more positive light. Example: *It's normal for people to need attention and affection. My parents could not meet my needs; that doesn't mean I was not an overly needy child.*

    _____

    _____

    _____

    _____

It's unrealistic to expect yourself to change a long-held belief in a few days or weeks, but with consistent practice you'll get there! I encourage you to repeat this exercise regularly to facilitate and notice how your thoughts change. You can also do this exercise with additional core beliefs. This exercise is available for download at this book's website, http://www.newharbinger.com/53905.

Reduce Estrangement-Related Shame

As we discussed in part 1, adult children receive a lot of negative messages about estrangement and themselves as people who chose to sever family ties. You've probably internalized some of these beliefs, which can contribute to you feeling ashamed of who you are and guilty about what you've done. However, measuring yourself against other people's beliefs and values is not an effective way to determine your worth as a person. We need to be clear about our own values, because when our actions align with our values we tend to feel good about ourselves, and if we're out of alignment, we know what changes we need to make. The next exercise will help you examine your beliefs about family relationships and estrangement and recognize how judgment creates feelings of shame.

Exercise: Clarify Your Beliefs and Recognize Your Worth

Take your time completing this chart. There aren't right or wrong answers, and being uncertain about your beliefs is okay. Most importantly, remember that other people's beliefs, values, and attitudes are not facts. We all get to decide for ourselves what we believe and how we feel about ourselves.

Beliefs to Consider	What You Believe	What Others Believe (Consider strong influences such as your parents, religious teachings, or society at large)
Adults who cut ties with their parents are…?	Example: *Strong, courageous, determined to break dysfunctional patterns*	Example: *Difficult, selfish, heartless*
Family is…?		
Estrangement is…?		
Adult children should interact with their parents by…?		
Adult children who feel mistreated by their parents should…?		

Boundaries are...?		
Mental health is...?		

How did clarifying your beliefs impact how you feel about yourself and your decision to distance yourself from your parents?

_____

_____

Choose a belief from the chart that increases feelings of self-worth and rewrite it here to reinforce its importance.

I believe _____

If it's helpful, you can use this statement as an affirmation when you're feeling low.

Final Thoughts

We tackled two challenging emotions—anger and shame—in this chapter. You practiced feeling uncomfortable emotions, finding healthy releases, changing inaccurate thoughts, and being kinder to yourself. Before we move on, pause to recognize how hard you're working and your commitment to healing. Next, we'll explore the importance of taking care of yourself as you continue to work toward healing.

CHAPTER 6

Taking Care of Yourself

As you know, family estrangement, and the trauma that typically precedes it, can have a profound impact on one's physical and emotional health. Self-care, which promotes healing and resilience, is an essential practice for dealing with estrangement challenges and related trauma. By cutting ties, you've taken a massive step to protect and care for yourself. In this chapter, we'll build on this with a discussion of what constitutes self-care, why it's important, and why adult children who are estranged from a family member often struggle with it. We'll conclude with some exercises and practical tips for prioritizing self-care.

Self-Care Aids Emotional Healing

Prioritizing self-care is always important, but even more so when you're stressed and asking a lot of yourself—as you are right now. Emotional healing can be a long, exhausting process. You might liken it to running ten miles every day. Both use a lot of your resources, and if you don't replenish them you'll become depleted, exhausted, physically sick, and discouraged; you won't have the energy and focus you need to persevere. By prioritizing self-care, you can heal, build resilience, and find a sense of peace amidst the turmoil. Every time you nurture yourself, you are changing long-held beliefs and patterns; you are courageously and intentionally caring for yourself in ways your family did not.

Self-care is the practice of tending to your physical, emotional, intellectual, social, and spiritual needs. It includes healthy habits and routines—things we do regularly to maintain our health, such as physical exercise and regular dental cleanings. Self-care also includes things we do periodically in response to a particular need. For example, calling a friend to vent after a difficult day or canceling plans when you're overwhelmed and need quiet time to de-stress.

Self-care includes:

- Setting boundaries

- Limiting your time on social media

- Getting a mammogram, colonoscopy, or other unpleasant medical test

- Quality time with your partner or friends

- Spending time alone

- Engaging in a hobby

- Treating yourself to something nice

- Limiting how much alcohol you drink

- Going to bed early when you're tired

- Maintaining a consistent bedtime

- Writing in a journal

- Exercising

- Connecting with your spiritual beliefs

- Spending time in nature

- Learning something new

- Forgiving yourself

- Taking medication as prescribed

Gentle Reminder: Self-care isn't always enjoyable, but it's always an act of self-love because we know it's good for us.

As you can see, self-care takes many forms. It varies from one person to the next due to our differing needs and preferences. Your self-care activities will change depending on what you need on a given day. Sometimes, self-care is enjoyable and feels good in the moment. Other times it's boring, unpleasant, or an investment in our future health. What's essential to self-care is that it's an activity that promotes healing.

Gentle Reminder: You can and should give yourself the love and care you didn't get from your parents.

How might you benefit from improved self-care?

_____

_____

_____

_____

Even when we know self-care is good for us, it's not always easy to do. Let's address some common barriers to practicing self-care before we embark on taking action.

Barriers to Self-Care

Self-care uses a variety of skills—recognizing and valuing your needs, self-discipline, setting boundaries, and self-compassion—that we ideally learn in childhood. However, if you didn't receive enough nurturing and structure as a child, you may not have learned these skills, so it's extra challenging to provide yourself self-care as an adult. Likewise, if your parents were overly harsh and controlling, you may have a hard time recognizing your needs as an adult because you were always told what to do and when to do it. We also learn about self-care by watching how our parents take care of themselves. For example, we often pick up unhealthy habits like smoking or people pleasing from our parents, as well as counterproductive attitudes about mental health care and self-compassion.

At its core, self-care is about recognizing your needs and meeting them. Unfortunately, many children grow up in families where their needs don't matter. Their needs are ignored, even when they cry out in pain or ask for help, comfort, or necessities. And when you realize your needs are irrelevant, you naturally stop paying attention to them. Furthermore, in families where there is addiction, abuse, or rage, children learn early on to cater to other people's needs as an act of self-preservation. Let's look at how Juan's and Mina's family dynamics affected their understanding of their needs, and then you can reflect on your own experiences.

• *Juan*

Juan's mother was frequently drunk, passed out, or preoccupied with her own needs and problems. So, his needs went unnoticed. Eventually, he stopped asking for anything, whether it was new shoes or attention, because he knew his mother wouldn't come through. It was easier and safer to act like he didn't need anything. Even as an adult, it's hard for him to do anything for himself because he doesn't think his needs are important. He works nonstop and can't say no without being flooded with guilt. Juan also struggles to maintain healthy habits because there weren't any consistent routines or good role models in his childhood. No one taught him basic self-care practices like how to cook healthy meals, create a soothing bedtime routine, or manage stress.

• *Mina*

Like Juan, Mina learned during childhood that her feelings and needs didn't matter. Her mother maintained a rigid schedule that Mina and her brothers followed, or they'd face their father's wrath. They did what they were told regardless of how they felt or what they wanted or needed. Even as a teenager, Mina had no autonomy to make decisions or change her routine to meet her needs. Even though some healthy habits, like brushing her teeth and wearing sunscreen, were drilled into her, she struggles to trust her emotions and treat herself with kindness.

What did you learn about self-care from your family of origin? Did your family model self-care and healthy habits? Were your parents attentive to your feelings and needs?

_____

_____

_____

_____

_____

_____

What makes it difficult for you to practice self-care?

_____

_____

_____

_____

I hope that being aware of these obstacles, and where they come from, increases your self-compassion. If you didn't learn how to practice self-care in childhood, it's not your fault. Fortunately, it's never too late to learn how to prioritize self-care!

How to Prioritize Self-Care

Prioritizing self-care is a big shift for folks who grew up thinking their needs don't matter or that they don't deserve self-care. To do so you need to change your mindset and your behaviors—and that can be daunting. To simplify the process, we're going to focus on six key elements:

- Recognize and value your needs.

- Establish healthy habits and routines.

- Start small.

- Be consistent.

- Lean on others.

- Set boundaries.

You'll find that these tasks overlap and are beneficial even if you only make small changes.

Recognize and Value Your Needs

Many people mistakenly believe that self-care must be earned or deserved. However, it's not a reward for working hard or being a good person. Self-care is simply about meeting normal human needs. Everyone has needs, so it's not realistic to expect yourself to work without getting tired or care for others and never need anything in return. Instead, try to normalize having needs, and remember that healthy, mature people take care of themselves and know their needs are as important as everyone else's. This can be a big change if you're used to putting everyone else's needs before your own. You may feel guilty or selfish when you practice self-care. This isn't because you're doing something wrong. It's because you're doing something unfamiliar or something that others discouraged you from doing, so they could take advantage of you.

Gentle Reminder: Everyone has needs and yours matter as much as everybody else's.

Noticing what you need takes practice. Listening to your emotions and body is a good place to begin. Often, we just need to slow down and tune in to what they're telling us. Being aware of common human needs can also be helpful. They include (adapted from Martin 2019):

- Food and water
- Physical activity
- Sleep
- Rest or relaxation
- Safety (physical and emotional)
- Play or recreation
- Belonging, social connection, and love
- Emotional well-being
- Stability
- Solitude or peace
- Sense of purpose
- Self-worth and a sense of competence
- Self-determination or autonomy
- Self-expression and creativity
- Connection to God, a higher power, the universe, or something larger than yourself
- Learning, knowledge, or understanding

Once you've identified a need, you can generate ideas for meeting it. Sometimes, the self-care activity that will meet your need is obvious, such as eating when you're hungry. Other times, it will take some trial and error. You'll want to consider what activities are feasible given the situation and your preferences. For example, Mina might meet her need for social connection by taking a cooking class, and Dan might spend quality time with his girlfriend.

Use the next exercise to practice identifying your needs and ways to meet them.

Exercise: Recognize Your Needs

Make an entry on this chart (adapted from Martin 2019) at least once per day. With practice, you'll be able to instinctively identify your needs without needing to use this chart. However, for now you'll need to be intentional in order to identify your needs. Consistency will be helpful; to remind yourself to fill out this chart daily, set a reminder on your phone or pair the task with a set activity, such as a meal. To continue practicing, you can download additional copies of this chart at the book's website, http://www.newharbinger.com/53905.

Date/Time	Emotions(s)	Body Sensation(s)	Need(s)	Ways to Meet Needs
Monday noon	Overwhelmed	Headache Tearful Jittery	Calm Confidence	Take a walk to clear my head. Ask Eshan to pick up the kids. Read affirmations.

Establish Healthy Habits and Routines

Healthy habits and routines are part of what I consider proactive—rather than reactive—self-care. They're consistent actions that we incorporate into our daily lives to maintain our health and well-being. Once established, habits become automatic (for example, drinking a glass of water when you wake up). A routine is a set of behaviors that we repeat often, such as a multistep bedtime routine. The power of healthy habits and routines lies in their cumulative effect; the more you practice them, the more they shape your overall well-being. Once established, habits and routines make it easier for us to make healthy choices. For example, you're more likely to meditate if it becomes a habit; you do it automatically without consciously deliberating whether you want to do it or not. Predictable routines also help us feel safe, which is especially important in trauma recovery.

With the needs you identified in the previous exercise in mind, choose two to three habits or routines you'd like to establish.

_____

_____

_____

How do you think they will improve your health or well-being?

_____

_____

_____

Start Small

People commonly make the mistake of attempting to make too many changes at once. When we do, we typically aren't very successful because we feel discouraged and quit. And even if we're initially successful, it's hard to maintain multiple new behaviors, so we drift back to our old patterns, which again create feelings of failure, and perhaps shame. In contrast, making smaller changes increases our chances of success, which keeps us motivated for the long haul. Caroline Arnold, the author of *Small Move, Big Change* (2014), suggests setting microgoals that are so specific and doable that you're certain you can achieve them. For example, if your goal is to keep your house neat, choose one small change you can make, say sorting your mail immediately rather than letting it collect on the kitchen counter. It's tempting to set your sights higher fearing that a small change like tackling the mail won't result in any significant change—and at first, it may not. But successfully making small shifts will motivate you to develop additional healthy habits that can really add up.

Using one of the desired habits or routines you identified in the preceding section, break this goal into smaller, more specific pieces. What's one small change you will make?

_____

How confident are you that you can achieve this goal?

_____

If you're less than 99 percent certain, break it into a more manageable expectation. Continue this process until you've got a goal that you're confident you can achieve.

_____

_____

_____

_____

Try to avoid all-or-nothing thinking that tells you that you must do it all and do it perfectly. Being overly rigid and setting impossibly high standards is counterproductive. Instead, focus on minor changes and celebrate your progress and effort. Even a small increase in self-care can have a significant impact and lead to bigger changes down the road. Most importantly, be gentle with yourself as you learn to tend to your needs.

Write a note of encouragement to remind yourself to have realistic expectations and to be kind to yourself when your self-care is imperfect.

_____

_____

_____

_____

> **Gentle Reminder:** Some self-care is better than none.

Be Consistent

Consistency turns good intentions into lasting change. As we've already discussed, setting realistic goals and breaking them down into manageable steps will help you be consistent, as will dedicating specific times for practicing your desired habits and routines.

When will you do this new behavior? Be as specific as possible.

_____

_____

Consistency also requires gentle accountability. You want to encourage yourself to stick to your self-care goals, but don't expect perfection. Setbacks are a natural part of the process, and it's normal to struggle with consistency. Instead of beating yourself up, use those moments as learning opportunities from which you can adjust your approach.

How can acknowledging your struggles and responding to them with kindness be motivating?

_____

_____

When you're inconsistent, what can you say or do to show yourself compassion?

_____

_____

Consistency is typically hard early in one's recovery. If you can't consistently practice healthy habits and routines now, that's okay. As you move through the healing process and your life gets more stable, you'll have more energy for establishing habits and routines. You can always revisit this section later.

Lean on Others

Building healthy habits and routines is easier, and sometimes more enjoyable, when we do it with a friend or supportive community. They can provide encouragement, tips, and accountability that will help you stay on track. Support can come from a variety of sources, and you can choose what's most useful for you, whether it's informal support from a friend; help from a professional, an accountability partner, or an app-based support; or joining an online or in-person group of individuals with similar goals. We'll talk more about how to find support in the next chapter.

Set Boundaries

Boundaries are limits that we set to protect something important. Communicating what we'll allow in our lives is a form of self-care that supports our need for respect, healthy relationships, and overall well-being. In addition, boundaries help us safeguard the time, money, energy, and other resources we need for self-care activities such as exercising, taking a vacation, or engaging in creative pursuits. Without boundaries, we run the risk of spending all or most of our resources meeting other people's needs and not having enough for ourselves. For example, scheduling time for self-care is a good start, but you need to protect it by communicating to others that you're not available for other activities during that time.

Setting boundaries is often uncomfortable even when we know it's in our own best interest. In my experience, people with weak boundaries tend to have big hearts and readily self-sacrifice—or feel guilty if they don't. You'll find that prioritizing self-care involves saying no or disappointing people sometimes. Generally, people who care about you will adjust when you set boundaries consistently and explain their role in self-care and healing. Setting boundaries doesn't mean that you don't care about others and their needs. It's about creating balance in your relationships such that your needs are as important as everyone else's.

Identify a self-care activity that you are likely to sacrifice when someone else objects to you spending time or money to do it or has a conflicting need.

_____

Describe how this situation might unfold. Whose needs would you be prioritizing? Why?

_____

_____

_____

_____

What boundaries could you establish that will help you meet your needs or prioritize self-care? Be as specific as possible.

_____

_____

_____

_____

If you need to communicate your boundaries to others, write a script and practice it to help yourself prepare for moments like these.

_____

_____

_____

_____

Do your best to communicate your boundaries with confidence, clarity, and warmth. And don't be discouraged if you sometimes feel guilty or uncertain. Like most things, setting boundaries gets easier the more you do it.

Final Thoughts

Self-care is a healing practice by which you give yourself the care your parents didn't. Valuing your needs aids the healing work you're doing today, and it will continue to be key to your health and happiness going forward. Even so, we can't meet all our needs ourselves. We also need support from others. Therefore, in the next chapter you'll consider how caring people can lighten your load and learn how to build a support network.

CHAPTER 7

Building a Support Network

Estrangement can leave you feeling isolated, overwhelmed, and wary of connection. However, you aren't alone. There are caring people who can truly understand your pain, and reaching out to them for emotional support can help you heal. That being said, building a support network isn't easy. In this chapter, you'll learn to navigate the challenges involved in building a support network, identify the types of support you need, take steps to strengthen your support network, and gain insights into how to talk about your estrangement. This chapter begins our discussion of developing and maintaining healthy relationships, which we'll expand upon in chapter 9.

The Importance of Support

When you're estranged from your parents, it's natural to feel an array of difficult emotions, such as grief, anger, guilt, and shame. These emotions can weigh heavily on you, making it crucial to have a support network. Building a network of individuals who understand your situation and provide emotional, practical, or professional support can make a world of difference.

> **Gentle Reminder:** Seeking support isn't a sign of weakness; it's a testament to your strength and resilience.

How Support Helps Us Heal

Although it may be tempting to try to handle your problems alone, interpersonal connections contribute to emotional healing in several important ways. Let's take a closer look at the benefits of social support.

- **Decreases isolation.** Connecting with empathetic people normalizes our experiences and fosters self-acceptance and understanding. Research shows that isolation has negative health effects, but satisfying interactions and meaningful connections can counteract these effects (see Holt-Lunstad et al. 2015; Lubben et al. 2015).

- **Improves mood, well-being, and coping abilities.** Emotional support helps people make sense of distressing experiences, facilitates positive change, and is associated with better mental health (Linden and Sillence 2021). It helps adult children build resiliency and cope with stress related to family estrangement (Dorrance Hall 2018; Hill and Gunderson 2015). Support groups for individuals experiencing family estrangement have been shown to reduce psychological distress and help participants feel less alone and ashamed (Blake, Bland, and Gilbert 2022).

- **Fosters hope.** Interacting with others who've successfully navigated the challenges of family estrangement allows us to envision a brighter future for ourselves. Their stories of growth and recovery demonstrate that healing is possible, and this can instill a sense of hope within us, encouraging us to persevere through our own healing journey.

- **Facilitates learning.** Building a support network allows us to learn from others who have faced similar struggles. We can exchange resources and coping strategies, observe how others handle difficult situations, and gain valuable insights and guidance. This collective wisdom and shared knowledge can enhance our healing process, empowering us to make informed choices and move forward.

How might social support aid your healing and overall well-being?

_____

_____

_____

_____

_____

Even when you recognize the benefits of building a support network, it's normal to feel apprehensive about doing it. Take a moment to acknowledge any lingering fears or concerns you have about asking for help from or connecting with others.

_____

_____

_____

_____

_____

The Challenges of Building a Support Network

Building a support network isn't easy, even in the best of times. And the effects of family estrangement and childhood trauma can make it extra challenging. However, understanding and acknowledging these obstacles can help you navigate them effectively and approach the process with patience and self-compassion. Let's explore some common challenges you may face as you work to establish your support network.

Loss of Supportive Relationships

Family estrangement often results in the loss of not only your familial connections but also friendships and other sources of support. Without the network of people who used to provide emotional support, you may find yourself feeling isolated. And putting in the time and emotional labor to strengthen existing relationships or form new ones can be daunting. For example, when Mina cut ties with her parents, she lost the support of her faith community, as her parents were members of the same temple.

Reluctance to Seek Support

As a result of growing up in a dysfunctional or abusive family, you may have developed "lone wolf tendencies"—that is, you are overly self-reliant, close yourself off emotionally, and avoid asking for help. It can be difficult to trust others and be vulnerable after the pain you've endured. The fear of being hurt, rejected, or abandoned again may make you hesitant to reach out for support. Overcoming this reluctance and finding the courage to seek help is a crucial step in your healing. For example, Juan couldn't rely on his mother growing up, so he learned that he could only trust himself. He was afraid to ask for help but found tremendous relief when he did.

Gentle Reminder: Asking for help is a sign of wisdom and strength. Everyone needs support.

Limited Resources

You may lack health insurance, have limited transportation options, or experience financial constraints that make it difficult to access the resources and services you need. Furthermore, there is a scarcity of support resources specifically designed for adult children experiencing family estrangement. This was the case for Dan, who was a college student when he cut ties with his parents. With no on-campus services for estranged students, and lacking the means to travel to a larger city to seek out support, he had to use what was available and found support through a campus LGBTQ+ organization.

Uncertainty About What You Need

It's common to feel uncertain about what kind of support would be most beneficial for your healing process. You may struggle to pinpoint exactly what you need and how to find it. This uncertainty adds to the challenge of seeking and obtaining support.

Consider your experiences seeking support. What's made it hard for you to build a robust support system or ask for help? Be specific.

_____

_____

_____

_____

_____

Remember, these challenges are not shortcomings or problems you caused. So, try not to criticize or judge yourself for needing help or struggling to get it. Instead, identifying obstacles can help you overcome them. Next, you'll identify what type of support you need and where you can find it.

Types of Social Support

Your support network will include multiple forms of support, each offering something different. As you read about the potential sources of support presented here, reflect on which types of support you might need. Your support needs will change as you heal, so you'll likely need different types of support as you progress.

Peer Support

Connecting with individuals who have experienced similar challenges can be invaluable. Peer support allows you to engage with other adult children who've been through family estrangement, providing an opportunity to share stories and resources and find a sense of understanding and validation. Interacting with peers who have walked a similar path can help you feel seen and heard in a powerful way.

To locate peer support, check local community centers, nonprofit organizations such as Together Estranged (US) and Stand Alone (UK), and therapists who facilitate support groups in your area. Because groups for adult children experiencing estrangement are limited, you may need to broaden your search to include peer support for other shared experiences, such as mental health challenges or abusive relationships, for example. Twelve-step groups for members of dysfunctional families can also be supportive; they include Co-Dependents Anonymous, Adult Children of Alcoholics and Dysfunctional Families, and Al-Anon. Twelve-step meetings are free and available in many locations, including online and via telephone.

Mental Health Support

Mental health professionals, such as therapists, counselors, social workers, and psychologists, support individuals experiencing an array of stressful situations, such as grief and life transitions, as well as people with ongoing mental health concerns. Therapists create emotional safety, which is key to healing from painful or traumatic experiences. They also use specific techniques to help clients decrease or manage bothersome symptoms and teach coping skills that can improve your mental health and relationships.

You can find a therapist using an online directory (suggestions are listed in the appendix), by asking your physician for a referral, or by asking a trusted friend or mentor if they know of a quality therapist. In the US, if you intend to use health insurance to pay for therapy, you can also locate a provider through your insurance plan directory or ask your employer's human resources department for assistance. Lower-cost counseling is available through Open Path Collective, local nonprofit counseling centers, university training programs, and public mental health departments. It's important to note that US therapists are licensed independently by each state.

So, you need to find a therapist who is licensed to practice in the state where you reside (even for telehealth services).

Online Communities

It's easy to connect with others, find resources, and share your story through online forums, chat groups, and social media groups. Although these forums can work well for some, others find it hard to make meaningful connections in groups that are unstructured, large, and lack face-to-face contact. If you're interested, look for groups that are well moderated; this feature will increase the emotional safety of the group.

Knowledge

There is a growing wealth of books, articles, podcasts, and online resources specifically focused on family estrangement and related topics. While these resources may not provide direct individual support or personal connections, they can help decrease feelings of isolation and shame, expand your understanding of family estrangement, and offer insights and perspectives that aid in your healing and growth.

Friends and Community

In addition to estrangement-specific support, you need people in your life who you can lean on and have fun with, and who make you feel valued and wanted. This type of support can come from friends, caring family members, mentors, and colleagues. Even if they don't fully understand the complexities of estrangement, their willingness to listen and support you can build meaningful connections that support your healing. And by engaging with your community, pursuing hobbies, and finding opportunities for enjoyment and connection you can build a fulfilling life.

Identify Your Support Needs

By understanding your needs and the types of social support available, you can create a support network that meets your unique needs. However, you can't do it all at once! Using a scale from 0 (no need or no existing support) to 10 (strong need or strong existing support), rate how much support you need and the strength of your existing support in each of the following areas. Your answers will help you prioritize what type of support to seek.

Support Type	Level of Need	Strength of Current Support
Peer Support		
Mental Health Support		
Online Communities		

Knowledge		
Friends and Community		
Other:		

Based on your needs, what type(s) of support will you work on finding now?

_____

_____

Next, you can create an action plan to find the support you need.

Exercise: Building Your Support Network

Building a support network takes consistent effort and intentional actions. To get started, identify three to five specific steps you'll take and when you'll do them. When creating your plan, consider ways to use or strengthen existing supports, as well as ways to add new resources and relationships. After you've accomplished some of your action items, you'll want to reflect on how they went and decide what next steps to take. Your plan is a work in progress! You can download a copy of this exercise at this book's website, http://www.newharbinger .com/53905.

Using and Strengthening Existing Supports	
Action Item	**When You'll Take Action**
Example: _Make a list of friends and acquaintances to reconnect with._	_November 1_

Finding New Resources and Making New Connections	
Action Item	**When You'll Take Action**
Example: *Search online for therapists and call two.*	*Tuesday during lunch break*

To help you get the support you need, let's consider *how* to talk with others about estrangement and other difficult experiences.

Tips for Building Your Support Network

- Meeting new people can feel less stressful if you focus on making connections rather than making friends.

- Cast a wide net and be open to connecting with people of diverse backgrounds and ages.

- Be open to trying something new. It's normal to feel nervous about trying something new because you don't know what to expect. On the other hand, you won't know if something—or someone—will be supportive if you don't give it a chance.

- Commit to attending groups or activities regularly. New situations may not immediately feel supportive as it takes time to develop trust, connection, and comfort with new people. As an introverted and generally anxious person, I know that new social situations are hard—and that they often get easier and more satisfying when I show up consistently.

- If something doesn't work for you, you can quit. I generally encourage folks to try a new thing two or three times before deciding it's not right for them. Give it time to work, but also trust your judgment and intuition. It's okay to change therapists, join a different group, or try another activity.

- Consider online support. You may not be able to find the support and services you need in your local area. Online support is often more accessible and affordable.

- If you can't find a support group that meets your needs, think about starting your own.

How to Talk About Estrangement

For many adult children, efforts to talk about family estrangement with friends and support people haven't gone well; instead they've increased feelings of shame and isolation rather than providing comfort and support. Therefore, I want to offer some tips on how to talk about family estrangement and ask for support in effective ways, while prioritizing your emotional well-being.

Be Selective

Not everyone in your support network may be equipped to handle conversations about family estrangement, and you should be discriminating about whom you share sensitive information with. Imagine that your support network consists of inner and outer circles. Those in your inner circle are your most trusted confidants. They've shown empathy, nonjudgmental attitudes, and good listening skills. They support you wholeheartedly. Your outer circle consists of casual friends and acquaintances. They're companions for activities and people with shared interests. You may chat with them about your day and share updates about new things happening in your life. However, these aren't people you'd feel comfortable confiding in regarding your innermost feelings, troubles, or secrets.

Who is in your inner circle?

_____

_____

_____

It's okay if your list is sparse. Most people only need a couple of close friends, and you can gradually build these relationships.

Who is in your outer circle?

_____

_____

_____

Set Boundaries

Boundaries communicate how we want to be treated and establish clear expectations in relationships. When sharing sensitive information, it's essential to set boundaries to protect your emotional well-being. You have the right to decide how much information you want to disclose and what you're comfortable discussing. Remember, you don't owe anyone a detailed explanation or justification for your choices. Clearly communicate your boundaries to members of your support network and ask that they respect them.

Here are some examples:

- *I tried for many years to make my relationship with my mom work. Please respect my decision.*

- *Please keep this conversation private.*

- *I'd rather not talk about that.*

What are some boundaries that you need to establish when talking to your support network about your family struggles?

_____

_____

_____

_____

_____

How can you make these requests in a kind yet firm manner? Try writing a script.

_____

_____

_____

_____

_____

Be Willing to Educate

Family estrangement is often misunderstood and mired in societal expectations and judgments. There may be folks in your life who could be supportive if they more fully understood family estrangement, its causes, and its effects. You might share with them information from this book or other reputable sources; sometimes statistics and expert opinions help people get a fuller, more balanced understanding of a phenomenon. When appropriate, provide information and encourage an open dialogue by inviting friends and acquaintances to ask questions. This creates an opportunity for growth, understanding, and more meaningful connections.

Which members of your support network might be interested in learning more about family estrangement?

_____

_____

_____

How can you help them learn more?

_____

_____

_____

Ask for What You Need

Gentle Reminder: Asking for what you need makes it easier for others to support you.

Before talking to your support network about your emotions, needs, or problems, take a moment to clarify what you need. Are you seeking validation, advice, a distraction from negative thoughts, or a listening ear? Understanding your needs will help you communicate them more effectively. Remember, your support network won't necessarily know what you need unless you express it.

Here are some examples of how to ask for what you need:

- *I know you mean well but I'm past trying to reconcile. What I need most is empathy and acceptance. Would you be willing to listen instead of offering advice?*

- *I know it's hard to understand but please trust that this is the best decision for me. You can support me by _____.*

Try writing some of your own.

_____

_____

_____

_____

_____

With practice, you'll get more comfortable and skilled at talking about estrangement and learn to discern who in your network is best suited to provide the support you need.

Creating a Chosen Family

As you develop close relationships with emotionally healthy individuals, you may create a "chosen family"—a group of people who choose to be a significant part of each other's lives through deep connection and a commitment to mutual support. In a chosen family, those who *act* like your family *are* your family. It's empowering and healing to create a family of your own choosing.

> **Gentle Reminder:** Family isn't defined by blood or legal ties. You get to decide who comprises your family.

A chosen family helps fill the void left by family estrangement. Chosen families may spend holidays together, go on vacation together, provide practical support, and act as a safety net. Some chosen families live together, and some do not. Some chosen families maintain a traditional family structure and use titles, such as mom or brother, to refer to each other. Others resemble a group of close friends. Most importantly, a chosen family is made up of people who deeply care about you and understand who you are and what you need. They celebrate your successes and walk with you through difficult experiences. Mina's and Juan's experiences are just two examples of the diversity of chosen families.

• *Mina*

Mina's elderly neighbors, Helen and Robin, are her chosen family. Their son is grown and lives across the country, so they relish the opportunity to be surrogate parents and grandparents to Mina and her daughter—babysitting, sharing meals, celebrating birthdays, and going to school functions. Helen's a great listener and a steady, calming presence in Mina's life. Mina's also a great help to them, running errands and providing companionship. Mina knows that she can count on Helen and Robin, and they can count on her!

• *Juan*

Juan was fortunate to have married into a warm, close-knit family. From the beginning, his in-laws welcomed him into the family and treated him with love and respect. They provided unconditional support throughout his struggles with his mother. They loaned him and his wife money to buy their home—and never made Juan feel bad for needing help. They also show an interest in his hobbies and cheer him on when he plays soccer. Their unconditional love has helped him heal and realize his self-worth.

A chosen family can emerge organically, or you may need to intentionally work on cultivating friendships. If the latter is true, download a copy of Tips for Meeting and Getting to Know People at this book's website, http://www.newharbinger.com/53905. It will help you get started.

How might you benefit from having a chosen family?

_____

_____

Who is or might be part of your chosen family?

_____

_____

_____

_____

What might you do to cultivate and sustain relationships with your chosen family?

_____

_____

_____

_____

Final Thoughts

Although it can be challenging work, building a support network has many benefits. Recognize that it's okay to ask for help and seek support from others who understand. Friends, support groups, mental health professionals, and online communities can all be a part of your support network. Remember, not everyone you reach out to will be the right fit for your needs. It's okay to try different approaches and to adjust your support network as you go along. Do your best to surround yourself with individuals who uplift and empower you, who respect your choices, and who support your growth. Over time, some members of your support network may evolve into a chosen family.

In the coming chapters, we'll focus on what it means to thrive and how you can create a fulfilling life. However, that doesn't mean your emotional healing is or should be finished. I encourage you to continue to use the materials in this section for as long as they're helpful. Healing is a gradual process, and it can overlap with the work we'll do in part 3, which begins with you exploring ways to live more authentically, and how doing so can increase well-being.

Part 3

Thriving

CHAPTER 8

Living Authentically

Cutting ties makes it possible for adult children to embark on a path of self-discovery, self-acceptance, and authentic living. In this chapter we'll explore what it means to live authentically, and why it's important, and go over strategies to help you live authentically and experience a life of purpose, joy, and fulfillment.

What Is Living Authentically?

When you live authentically, you know who you are and what you want and need, and you can fully express yourself and live according to your values and priorities. Family and societal expectations don't constrain you, so you're free to shine. Living authentically entails:

- Knowing who you are and what's important to you

- Being proud of all facets of your identity

- Feeling safe to be yourself

- Expressing yourself without fear or compromise

- Recognizing your strengths

- Having the courage to be different

- Not changing yourself to please others or to fit in

- Staying true to your values even if others disagree with them

- Prioritizing your needs

Living authentically involves aligning your actions, beliefs, and values with your genuine self, as well as introspection, self-awareness, and the willingness to confront and shed the layers of conditioning and self-doubt that have accumulated from the developmental trauma and dysfunctional relationships you've experienced.

What does living authentically mean to you?

_____

_____

The Importance of Living Authentically

Dysfunctional family dynamics impede our ability to develop a strong sense of self. To survive childhood, you probably had to conform to your parents' expectations to appease them, making it impossible for you to live authentically. This may have included giving up your own goals and adopting those of your parents', ending relationships that they didn't approve of, compromising your values, hiding parts of yourself, pretending to share their beliefs, being afraid to assert your opinions or needs, not trying new things, and not having the opportunity to explore your interests and identity.

Gentle Reminder: Living authentically empowers us to live fulfilling, purposeful lives.

Your desire to live authentically may have been one of the reasons you cut ties with your family of origin. After cutting ties, some adult children feel liberated from their parents' judgments, expectations, and limiting beliefs and can immediately start living more authentically. For others, living authentically evolves gradually. You may still be realizing how restricted you've been, how much parent pleasing you've done, and how you've abandoned your true self to be the person your parents want you to be.

When you live according to your values, you're likely to feel greater happiness, fulfillment, and a sense of purpose. You're more likely to feel confident about your decisions and actions because you aren't trying to be someone you aren't. This can lead to a more positive self-image and a greater sense of self-worth. Being able to express yourself authentically fosters self-acceptance and self-love, leading to increased self-confidence and a stronger sense of identity. Living authentically can also help you cultivate meaningful and deep connections with others, as you attract like-minded individuals who appreciate and embrace your true self. In addition, when you live authentically, you're less likely to feel stressed or anxious because you don't have to "mask" yourself or maintain a facade. You can relax and be your true self with certainty about who you are and what matters to you. Let's look at Mina's and Dan's experiences of living authentically.

Gentle Reminder: Knowing yourself is an essential step to loving yourself and feeling loved by others. You must show up authentically and be known and understood to feel loved.

• *Mina*

For over thirty years, Mina tried to be a perfect daughter. Her father was strict and controlling and she was understandably afraid to cross him. To cope, she tried to be who her parents wanted her to be. Mina wasn't allowed to express her own opinions or beliefs, she gave up her educational and career aspirations, and she was constantly made to feel guilty for not being perfect. It wasn't until after she cut ties that she recognized all that she'd given up and how out of touch with herself she was. Mina had no hobbies, and her romantic relationships and friendships were shallow and unfulfilling because she didn't understand herself and her needs, nor did she voice her opinions and feelings. She'd chalked this up to being a busy, single mother but now realized it was largely because she'd prioritized her parents' needs and values over her own.

After cutting ties, she could try things her parents didn't approve of and gained confidence in articulating her thoughts, opinions, and emotions without fear of judgment or retribution. This enabled her to build more fulfilling relationships. Mina identified a cause close to her heart—environmental conservation—and threw herself into volunteering for local environmental organizations, attending rallies, and promoting sustainable practices. By aligning herself with this cause, Mina found a sense of purpose and fulfillment, contributing to positive change while becoming friends with like-minded individuals who shared her values. Freed from the constraints imposed by her parents, Mina pursued her career aspirations. She enrolled in courses related to environmental science and sustainability, eager to gain knowledge and skills that would enable her to have a meaningful impact in her chosen field. With her newfound independence, Mina felt empowered to advance her professional goals and build a better future for herself and her daughter.

• *Dan*

Dan's desire to live authentically was central to his decision to sever ties with his parents. His parents didn't accept his gender identity and often made him feel ashamed of who he is. They tried to prevent him from expressing himself in ways that align with his gender, and they constantly misgendered him. Dan's parents' rejection took a toll on his mental health. He became depressed and isolated, and he started to doubt his worth. He felt like he could never be genuinely happy if he couldn't live authentically.

After cutting ties with his parents, Dan was finally free to be himself. He found joy and liberation in expressing himself authentically, allowing his appearance and style to reflect who he truly is. This newfound freedom allowed him to build a stronger sense of self and navigate the world with increased confidence. He got involved in the LGBTQ+ community, and through support groups, social events, and advocacy work he found a group of supportive friends who shared similar experiences and challenges. By immersing himself in his community, Dan found understanding, acceptance, and a sense of true belonging, further strengthening his sense of identity and purpose.

What do you relate to in Mina's or Dan's stories?

_____

_____

_____

_____

How have you compromised or restricted yourself to try to please or appease your parents?

_____

_____

_____

_____

How has living inauthentically negatively affected you?

_____

_____

_____

_____

What would living more authentically look like?

_____

_____

_____

_____

How might living authentically improve your health or well-being?

_____

_____

Five Ways to Live Authentically

Now, let's explore five aspects of living authentically—self-discovery, self-acceptance, self-expression, authentic connections, and living with purpose—and steps you can take to create a life that reflects your authentic self.

Self-Discovery

The first step to living authentically is to get to know yourself better. Once you have a better understanding of who you are and what's important to you, you can start to live in a way that is more aligned with your true self. Self-discovery is a process of self-reflection, trying new things, and figuring out who you are and how you want to live. Ask yourself what truly matters to you and what brings you a sense of fulfillment. Self-discovery often includes identifying your core values—the principles and beliefs that are most important to you. Take time to reflect on what resonates with you and what you stand for.

> **Gentle Reminder:** Self-reflection helps you stay true to your values and goals and ensures that your choices are in alignment with the life you want to live.

You can start your self-discovery work with the following exercise. Self-discovery is an ongoing process, and I encourage you to continue to reflect on these questions in the coming weeks and months. You can download a printable copy of this exercise at this book's website, http://www.newharbinger.com/53905.

Exercise: Self-Discovery

Identify some of your goals.

_____

_____

_____

_____

Identify some of your values.

_____

_____

_____

_____

Identify some of your beliefs.

_____

_____

_____

_____

Identify some of your interests.

_____

_____

_____

_____

Identify some things you like, that give you pleasure, or that energize you.

_____

_____

_____

_____

Identify some things you dislike, you don't want to be a part of, or that deplete your energy.

_____

_____

_____

_____

Identify four to five strengths or personal traits that you value in yourself. If identifying personal strengths is a challenge, consider what strengths or traits you value in others.

_____

_____

_____

_____

What is most important to you? How do you know?

_____

_____

_____

_____

In addition to answering these questions, try engaging in activities that encourage self-reflection, such as journaling, meditation, or therapy. Experiment with new activities and allow yourself to embrace the aspects of your identity that you've suppressed or overlooked in the past.

What other self-discovery activities will you engage in to help you understand yourself better?

_____

_____

_____

_____

Self-Acceptance

Once you know who you are, you can work toward self-acceptance. *Self-acceptance* is the belief that all aspects of your identity are valid and worth celebrating. Remember, authenticity is not about perfection; it's about embracing your entire self, including your flaws and shortcomings. When you accept yourself, you feel confident; you don't need to prove yourself or earn people's love and approval.

Self-acceptance is similar to the concept of self-worth discussed in chapter 5. If you experienced rejection, disapproval, or harsh criticism in your family of origin, self-acceptance includes unlearning the limiting beliefs instilled in you by your family, deprogramming the inner critic they installed in your head, and treating yourself with the unconditional love they failed to provide. Like many of the growth-oriented strategies we've discussed, accepting yourself may feel uncomfortable at first. With consistent effort, self-acceptance will come more naturally. Remember, self-acceptance isn't all or nothing; small changes can have a big impact on your happiness. Here are two exercises to help you practice self-acceptance. I hope you'll give both a try!

Exercise: Self-Talk for Self-Acceptance

Identify a current struggle or something you have a tough time accepting about yourself, such as a worry, mistake, or personal trait.

Examples:

> *Yelling at my children*
>
> *Family estrangement*

Using the prompts below, write a statement that describes your issue followed by a statement of self-acceptance.

Examples:

> *Even though I yelled at my children, I completely accept myself.*
>
> *Even though I'm not in contact with my father, I love and accept myself.*

You can also use the phrase "I'm *learning* to accept myself," if it feels more authentic.

Even though I _____, I

_____.

Place your hands over your heart or gently stroke your cheeks and say your statement aloud four times. Alternatively, write it several times in the space provided, or in a journal.

_____

_____

_____

Repeat your affirming statement several more times throughout the day. I also find it helpful to write self-affirming statements like these on notecards and place them in visible areas, such as taped to my bathroom mirror or desk, to reinforce the belief that I accept myself.

Exercise: Self-Acceptance Through Mindfulness

Mindfulness is a tool that can facilitate greater self-acceptance. It's the practice of being present focused and tuning in to ourselves and our surroundings. It helps us notice our thoughts, emotions, personality traits, and behaviors without judging them. Through mindfulness, we can practice accepting ourselves just as we are and learn to appreciate things about ourselves and our lives that might otherwise go unnoticed or be sources of discontent or self-criticism.

This exercise (based on Brach 2019; Neff and Germer 2018) will help you harness the therapeutic benefits of mindfulness and self-compassion. You can download a printable copy of this exercise at this book's website, http://www.newharbinger.com/53905. You can do this exercise at any time but may find it easiest and most impactful when something is bothering you or you're having a tough time. Allow yourself five to ten minutes without distractions.

1. **Notice and name your emotions.** By noticing our emotions we bring awareness to important insights about ourselves, and naming them helps us clarify what we're feeling and how we want to respond. What emotions are you experiencing? Be specific.

_____

_____

_____

2. **Observe physical sensations.** Emotions also manifest physically, and we can learn a lot by paying attention to our bodies. How does your body feel? For example, you might notice tension in your neck or shoulders, tightness in your chest, butterflies in your stomach, or pain somewhere specific.

_____

_____

_____

3. **Accept what is.** Let your thoughts, feelings, and experiences exist without judgment or trying to change or avoid them. This step takes courage, as you're asking yourself to be completely honest about what you're experiencing and to release your desire to change what is. What are you allowing or accepting?

_____

_____

_____

4. **Explore.** Be curious about your experiences by asking yourself: Why do I feel this way? What are these physical sensations telling me? What else might be going on? What else am I noticing?

_____

_____

_____

5. **Release and self-soothe.** Let go of difficult emotions by relaxing your body and treating yourself with compassion. What do you need? How can you nurture yourself? This might include saying something kind or reassuring to yourself or hugging or massaging yourself, or some other form of gentle touch.

_____

_____

_____

6. **Reflect.** How did it feel to accept yourself? What did you learn about yourself? How did it feel to release and self-soothe?

_____

_____

_____

Tips for Practicing Self-Acceptance

- Avoid comparing yourself to others.

- Limit time on social media.

- Avoid people who put you down or treat you poorly.

- Set realistic expectations for yourself; don't expect perfection.

- When you make a mistake or fall short, be kind to yourself. Mistakes are learning opportunities.

- Celebrate your progress and effort, not just the outcome.

- Say kind things to yourself.

- Accept compliments and praise, but don't rely on them to feel good about yourself.

- Prioritize self-care.

- Treat yourself with love and respect.

- Use positive affirmations or mantras, such as "I am enough" or "I don't have to prove my worth."

Self-Expression

One of the most liberating aspects of living authentically is having the freedom to express yourself fully. In your family of origin, you may have suppressed aspects of your identity, as well as your thoughts, feelings, and desires, due to the fear of being shamed or rejected. Now you can reclaim your voice and express yourself authentically. We can express ourselves through writing, speaking, art, music, dance, dress, appearance, personal style, or any activity that communicates who we are and what we believe.

Self-expression can be public or private; both are equally valid. Some adult children who are estranged from family members grow more comfortable with expressing themselves publicly as they heal. Others are naturally more private. You don't need to pressure yourself to express yourself in ways that feel uncomfortable. What's important is that you find healthy and constructive ways to express yourself without inhibition.

In what ways can you express yourself authentically?

_____

_____

_____

_____

Authentic Connections

Authentic relationships tend to be deep and meaningful. They're built on a foundation of mutual respect and acceptance and involve allowing yourself to be seen and heard. Being vulnerable—sharing your thoughts, feelings, dreams, and fears—isn't easy because it's not something you could safely do with your family of origin. You may find that you're guarded in relationships as a way to protect yourself from potential hurt and rejection. However, when we're open and honest with others, we build trust and connection.

Work on building authentic connections slowly by gradually sharing more of yourself with others as trust and connection develop. Sharing your feelings, opinions, ideas, worries, and dreams with trusted friends, family members, or a therapist—rather than just anyone you know or meet—is a safer way to begin building authentic connections. Support groups and communities in which you can express yourself authentically are also good options for building authentic connections early in your recovery.

What's one thing you can do this week to build an authentic connection with someone in your life?

_____

_____

What's one thing you can do next week?

_____

_____

Following through with these goals will be a great start to building authentic relationships! In the next chapter you'll learn more about creating healthy relationships.

Living with Purpose

Authentic living involves aligning your actions with your values and priorities. When you live with purpose, you spend most of your time, energy, and resources on whatever's most important to you. Doing so will give you a deeper sense of fulfillment, meaning, and satisfaction in your life. To live with purpose, you need to understand what matters to you and make conscious choices that align your actions with your values and priorities.

To begin, take what you've learned about yourself through the exercises in this chapter and go deeper, focusing on what you feel strongest about. Then, consider how, and to what extent, you're putting your passions and values into action. As with most things, it's easiest to start with a small action. For example, if education is a value you hold strongly, you don't need to become a teacher or join the school board to live with purpose. You might volunteer to tutor students at a local school or donate to organizations that promote literacy. Living with purpose is not a single action, but the result of consistently aligning your values and behaviors. So, be sure to consider a variety of ways to act on your priorities.

What do you feel most passionate about? What drives or fulfills you?

_____

_____

_____

_____

_____

What values and beliefs define who you are at your core?

_____

_____

_____

_____

_____

How are you putting your passions and values into action?

_____

_____

_____

_____

_____

How might your life be different if it were more aligned with your values and priorities?

_____

_____

_____

_____

_____

Final Thoughts

Distancing yourself from your parents has made it possible for you to live authentically. If you're already living more fully as your true self, be sure to celebrate how far you've come. You are uniquely wonderful and important. By living authentically, you can create a life that is truly your own—one that is free of the chains of toxicity and full of joy, fulfillment, and love. If you're just beginning your journey of self-discovery, take your time and allow yourself to explore and experiment. In time, you'll feel more comfortable and confident, knowing who you are and feeling free to be yourself and make your own choices. I hope you'll continue this work as we move forward with our discussion of healthy relationships in the next chapter.

CHAPTER 9

Developing Healthy Relationships

Relationships are an essential part of a fulfilling life. Healthy relationships—with friends, romantic partners, roommates, coworkers, neighbors, and others—provide a safe and supportive space for us to grow and thrive together. However, many adult children who are estranged from family members reach adulthood with few models and experiences of healthy relationships. Trying to develop healthy relationships without any guidance can be scary, confusing, and frustrating. So, in this chapter we'll start by identifying the defining features of healthy relationships to help you clarify what healthy relationships mean to you and what they would look like in your life. Then we'll address how to build trust and mutuality, come to understand our emotional triggers so we can respond rather than react, identify deal-breakers, and determine how to handle unhealthy relationships.

Identify and Create Healthy Relationships

Healthy relationships are based on mutual respect, trust, and honest communication. When you're in a healthy relationship, you feel understood, supported, and appreciated. You're able to express your feelings and needs openly, and you feel safe and secure in the relationship.

Characteristics of a healthy relationship include:

- Trust

- Mutual respect

- Honesty

- Emotional and physical safety

- Open and honest communication

- Addressing conflicts

- Apologizing or making amends

- Compromise

- Empathy

- Care and nurturing

- Play and fun

- Acceptance

- Mutual support of needs, goals, and interests

Learning to create healthier relationships can feel overwhelming, especially if you've only ever known dysfunctional family relationships. Remember, healthy relationships exist on a continuum. Your goal is to build healthier—not perfect—relationships, and even small steps in that direction can improve your well-being. Here are some things you can do to move toward the goal of having healthier relationships.

Be selective: The first step to creating healthier relationships is choosing people who are interested in and capable of having healthy relationships. As you know, not everyone is. Put a checkmark next to the items that resonate with you, and add your own ideas in the blank spaces. Look for people who:

- ☐ Own their mistakes, admit when they're wrong, and apologize

- ☐ Are empathetic

- ☐ Are interested in your well-being, ideas, feelings, goals, and interests

- ☐ Show appreciation

- ☐ Respect others' boundaries

- ☐ Can be vulnerable

- ☐ Prioritize their mental health and well-being

- ☐ Approach conflict with respect and care

- ☐ Accept you as you are

- ☐ Regulate their emotions

- ☐ Have an open mind and are willing to learn

- ☐ Are patient

- ☐ Ask for what they need

- ☐ _____

- ☐ _____

Communicate effectively: Develop effective communication skills, both for expressing yourself and actively listening to others. Avoid assumptions and be transparent about your feelings and expectations.

Set boundaries: Boundaries are agreements about how people will treat each other; they keep us safe, and they establish clear expectations in relationships. Clarify what you are and are not comfortable with, and communicate your boundaries early on in any relationship. In addition, you must try to respect other people's boundaries.

Be willing to compromise: Sometimes people have conflicting needs and compromise allows both parties to get most of their needs met most of the time. Be mindful that you aren't doing all of the giving or all of the taking in a relationship. Compromise is about finding solutions that work for both people.

Prioritize quality time: We're all busy, and, as a result, sometimes we neglect our relationships. Relationships need to be nurtured, and quality time creates stronger emotional connections. Jointly, plan how and when you'll spend time together.

Create a supportive environment: Encourage your friends' and partner's personal growth and aspirations. Show interest in their goals and interests. Celebrate their successes and provide comfort during challenging times.

Allow yourself to be vulnerable: As trust develops, share more of your authentic self—your emotions, insecurities, fears, and hopes. Likewise, show empathy and be emotionally available to support and listen to your friends' and partner's concerns and feelings.

Resolve conflicts constructively: When conflicts arise, approach them as opportunities for growth. Focus on finding solutions instead of assigning blame.

Show appreciation: Regularly express gratitude and appreciation for the people in your life. Small gestures of kindness can go a long way in nurturing healthy relationships.

Be willing to work on relationships: Maintaining healthy relationships takes effort. There will be difficulties, and both people in a relationship need to be willing to resolve conflicts, be vulnerable, and overcome challenges. If you are struggling with a relationship, a therapist or counselor can help you individually or jointly by providing guidance and skills to improve it.

> **Gentle Reminder:** Healthy relationships are physically and emotionally safe.

Describe what a healthy relationship means to you.

_____

_____

_____

_____

What would a healthy friendship look like?

_____

_____

_____

_____

What would a healthy romantic relationship look like?

_____

_____

_____

_____

If you have or plan to have children, what would a healthy relationship with your children look like?

_____

_____

_____

_____

How would these relationships be different from the ones you've had previously?

_____

_____

_____

_____

Learn to Trust

Trust is an essential component of healthy relationships. It's the foundation upon which emotional intimacy, open communication, and a sense of safety are built. Without trust, misunderstandings, conflicts, and emotional distance are more likely. Trust allows us to be vulnerable with each other, knowing that our thoughts and feelings will be respected and protected.

Gentle Reminder: Remaining emotionally closed off feels safe but prevents you from connecting with others.

When people in your life mistreat you—are critical, manipulative, rejecting, unpredictable, or violent—you learn that people can't be trusted, to expect the worst from them, and to be on guard. Not trusting was an important survival skill in your family of origin. So, it makes sense that you may be reticent to trust others. Or you may struggle with the other end of the spectrum—trusting too easily. You may trust people you don't know well or who don't have your best interest at heart. Trusting too much or too little impedes our ability to have healthy relationships. When we don't trust, we can't receive comfort and experience the joys of being known and understood by others. And trusting too easily can lead to us being taken advantage of or hurt by others.

Describe a time when you struggled to trust someone or be vulnerable. How did your difficulty trusting affect you and the relationship?

_____

_____

_____

_____

_____

Describe a situation when you trusted too easily. How did doing so affect you?

_____

_____

_____

_____

_____

The next exercise can help you determine how trustworthy someone is. You can download additional copies at this book's website, http://www.newharbinger.com/53905, and repeat the exercise to assess your level of trust in different relationships.

Exercise: Trust Assessment

Answer the following questions with a specific person in mind. Your assessment will be more accurate if you consider multiple encounters with this person rather than gauging their trustworthiness based on a single point in time.

Are they consistent? Is their behavior predictable? Do they do what they say they're going to do and fulfill their commitments?

_____

_____

_____

Are they reliable? Can you count on them to be there when needed? Do they show up, both in good times and bad, and offer support and care?

_____

_____

_____

Are they honest? Are they truthful and forthcoming, even when the truth might be difficult to share?

_____

_____

_____

Are they accountable? Do they take responsibility for their actions and acknowledge their mistakes? Do they strive to make amends and learn from their errors?

_____

_____

_____

Do they behave with integrity? Do they value honesty and accountability? Do they treat others with respect?

_____

_____

_____

Do they respect your boundaries and limits? When you say no, do they pressure you to change your mind or behavior, or to disclose more than you feel comfortable sharing?

_____

_____

_____

Are they interested in your experiences and feelings? Do you feel heard, valued, and affirmed by them?

_____

_____

_____

Take some time to reflect on your answers. What conclusions can you draw about this person's trustworthiness?

_____

_____

_____

Relationships are a two-way street, so you also need to do your part to build trust. You can ask the same questions of yourself to make sure you're a trustworthy friend or partner and adjust your behavior as needed. The following list includes additional actions you can take. Place a checkmark next to any items that are challenging for you or that you'd like to improve upon.

- ☐ Continue to develop self-trust. You may find it helpful to revisit the information on developing self-trust in chapter 2. Doing so will help you honor your emotions and listen to your instincts. As you develop self-trust, you can extend trust to others at a pace that feels comfortable to you.

- ☐ Open up gradually; it takes time to develop trust. Try to share more of your feelings and vulnerabilities as you begin to feel more safe. Doing so will build emotional intimacy.

- ☐ Show your friends and partner that they can rely on you by following through on your promises and by being consistent in your actions.

- ☐ Establish clear boundaries so others know what to expect from you and how you want to be treated.

- ☐ Communicate openly and honestly about your thoughts, feelings, and needs.

☐   Pay attention to your gut feelings and bodily sensations. Don't ignore red flags or your instincts telling you that something's off or someone may not be trustworthy.

☐   Don't expect others to be perfect. Consider offering a second chance if the other person shows remorse and a commitment to change. Please note that this doesn't mean offering unlimited chances or absolving others of their responsibilities. We'll talk more about this later in this chapter.

With a specific relationship in mind, list some action steps that you will take to help develop trust.

_____

_____

_____

_____

_____

> **Gentle Reminder:** Be patient with yourself. Learning whom to trust and allowing yourself to be vulnerable takes time and effort, especially after experiencing relational trauma.

Build Mutuality in Relationships

Growing up in a dysfunctional family predisposes adult-children to have one-sided relationships in which they give more than they receive. They become practiced at catering to other people's emotions and needs. They're quick to give in when conflict emerges. And they're willing to give up what they want or need to make others happy or avoid disappointing or enraging them. One-sided relationships are unfulfilling and often fraught with conflict, whereas healthy relationships are mutually supportive. Let's look at Mina's experience in a one-sided relationship.

•   *Mina and Rose*

Mina met Rose at work a year ago and they became fast friends. Rose was going through a difficult divorce and desperately needed a supportive friend. Mina could relate to Rose's struggles as she'd divorced a few years earlier. She spent many hours listening to Rose vent about her husband, researching affordable divorce attorneys, and coaching Rose on how to navigate the court process. Mina loaned Rose money and treated her to meals and movies, even though it meant putting off some needed car repairs. Mina initially felt good about helping Rose; they had fun together and it was a needed distraction from her own problems. However, as Mina's relationship with her parents deteriorated, she needed emotional support and practical help but was reluctant to ask Rose for help because she knew Rose was already feeling stressed. Rose seemed unaware of Mina's struggles and rarely asked how she was doing or offered support.

Have you had one-sided relationships like Mina's, in which you give and the other person doesn't reciprocate? Alternatively, unbalanced relationships aren't always due to a friend or partner being unwilling to offer support and care. Sometimes, we have difficulty asking for and accepting support and help when it's offered. This is common among adult children who are estranged from their parents because they learned in childhood that asking for help or depending on others leads to disappointment.

Gentle Reminder: Adult children often feel safer and more comfortable giving than receiving. Although generosity is a wonderful quality, one-sided relationships are not healthy or sustainable. You must give and receive support, respect, and care.

What have one-sided relationships looked like in your life? How have they impacted you?

_____

_____

_____

_____

_____

_____

_____

In healthy relationships, there's a give and take. We need to give and receive support. We need to show others they matter to us, and we need to feel that they value and appreciate us.

Tips for Balanced Relationships

- Explicitly ask for what you need or want. Don't assume that others know. And don't assume that they will say no.

- Prioritize meeting your own emotional needs by offering yourself the same love and care that you give to others.

- Set clear boundaries so that you and your friends and partners know what to expect. Boundaries demonstrate respect for yourself and others.

- Consider your options. Unfortunately, not all one-sided relationships can be improved. If you've repeatedly asked a friend or partner for support, help, or attention and they can't or won't provide it, you must carefully consider whether to continue the relationship.

Recognizing that a relationship is one-sided can be painful, and deciding how to proceed can feel overwhelming. Later in this chapter I'll discuss how to determine when to continue or end troubled relationships.

> **Gentle Reminder:** Asking for what you need involves being vulnerable. But it increases the chances that your needs will be met in a relationship, which leads to more satisfying relationships.

Understand Your Emotional Triggers

Emotional triggers are internal or external cues that remind you of traumatic experiences. They are natural and common responses, but left unchecked they can derail the healthy relationships you're building. When old wounds are irritated, you're likely to overrespond (have big, out-of-control, or overwhelming emotions) or underrespond (emotionally shut down) to the current situation. This doesn't mean your feelings aren't valid, but that they're rooted in wounds that run deeper than the distress caused by the current stressor (Campbell 2022). Others will inevitably say and do things that aggravate old wounds. This is why it's crucial to recognize your emotional triggers and process your feelings before responding. By learning to respond to emotional triggers rather than react, you can decrease hurt feelings and miscommunication in your relationships.

Exercise: Respond Rather Than React

This exercise is best done as soon as you feel emotionally triggered. However, if you don't recognize a trigger until after you've acted on it, you can use this exercise to reflect on what happened.

Briefly describe who or what triggered you.

_____

_____

_____

_____

What old wound was irritated by this experience?

_____

_____

_____

_____

Describe your emotions and physical sensations.

_____

_____

_____

_____

Spend ten to twenty minutes engaging in self-soothing activities (exercise, journaling, listening to music, meditating, or anything else of your choosing). Afterward, describe your thoughts and feelings.

_____

_____

_____

_____

_____

How would you like to respond to the situation that triggered you?

_____

_____

_____

What might you say or do to help the other person understand your experience or reaction? Or, if this event didn't involve another person, how might you safeguard yourself from this stressor in the future?

_____

_____

_____

What will you do to further heal this emotional wound?

_____

_____

_____

_____

You can download additional copies of this exercise at this book's website, http://www.newharbinger .com/53905. Continued practice will help you break unhealthy relationship patterns and learn to respond more effectively to stressors in the present moment.

Know Your Deal-Breakers

When two people are committed to having a mutually satisfying relationship, communicating your deal-breakers can head off problems and preserve the relationship. Healthy relationships involve compromise and flexibility, yet we all have deal-breakers, behaviors we cannot tolerate in a relationship. Deal-breakers protect us and ensure that our relationships meet our needs, so it's essential that you're clear about what's nonnegotiable for you. Mina's story shows why deal-breakers matter.

• *Mina*

Before her estrangement, Mina lacked boundaries with her parents and friends, which allowed them to take advantage of her. Reflecting on this, she identified deal-breaker behaviors that she didn't recognize at the time. When she began dating, she prioritized telling potential partners how she wanted to be treated and what would not be tolerated to avoid repeating past mistakes. Mina established deal-breakers such as zero tolerance for aggression, threats, derogatory names, or jeopardizing her physical safety.

Establishing deal-breakers is often a struggle for adult children who are estranged from family members due to the relational trauma they experienced in their family of origin. You may overcompensate by creating a long list of deal-breakers because it makes you feel safe. However, in reality, too many deal-breakers can cause you to unnecessarily cut people out of your life—leaving you isolated—when a compromise might be possible. Instead, aim to have four to five nonnegotiable boundaries in a specific relationship. Focus on behaviors that are so egregious that you're not willing to give someone a second chance if they behave this way. Typically, these are behaviors that compromise your health or safety (or the health and safety of your minor children).

Identify your deal-breakers. Be as specific as possible.

_____

_____

_____

_____

_____

Now that you know what your deal-breakers are, you can try to be flexible and open to compromise on other issues you find challenging or troubling.

When a Relationship Isn't Healthy

As you've been reading this chapter, you may have come to realize that some of your relationships aren't as healthy as you'd like them to be. You may be wondering whether a troubled relationship can be improved or if you're better off ending it. These are complex questions and there's no one-size-fits-all answer. You'll want to consider factors such as the nature and length of the relationship. Usually, we invest more effort into trying to save closer, longer-term relationships, such as one with a partner than say with a friend of three months. However, as you know from your experiences with your family of origin, sometimes even committed long-term relationships can't be transformed into functional relationships, and it's healthiest to walk away.

In conjunction with what you've already learned about healthy relationships, the following exercise can help you assess the health of a relationship and determine whether it makes sense for you to invest more energy into trying to improve it. You can download additional copies at this book's website, http://www.newharbinger .com/53905.

Exercise: Troubled Relationship Reflection

Do you feel physically and emotionally safe around this person? (Remember, safety is an essential component of a healthy relationship.)

_____

_____

_____

Is there equity in this relationship?

_____

_____

_____

How is this relationship negatively impacting you?

_____

_____

_____

_____

How does this relationship enhance your life? What are the benefits of continuing this relationship?

_____

_____

_____

_____

How is this relationship affecting important people in your life, such as your children?

_____

_____

_____

_____

What do you think will happen if the relationship continues on its current trajectory?

_____

_____

_____

_____

Are both parties invested in change efforts?

_____

_____

_____

_____

What do your answers tell you about the health of this relationship? What does your gut tell you?

_____

_____

_____

_____

When to Give a Second Chance

Sometimes, it makes sense to give people a second chance. We all make mistakes, and conflict and emotional hurt occasionally occur even in healthy relationships. You may find that you give people too many chances to change their behavior and get taken advantage of or hurt in the process. Or you may be quick to end relationships and refuse to give second chances regardless of the situation. There are many factors to consider when discerning whether to give a person another chance. Here are some:

- Is this hurtful behavior a one-off or part of a pattern?

- If it's a pattern, how long has it been going on? Is the behavior getting better or worse?

- Is the other person aware of the hurt they've caused and remorseful?

- What have they done to make amends? Are their efforts satisfactory?

- What have they done to change their behavior? Is it adequate?

- How serious is the issue? Is this a violation of a deal-breaker boundary?

- What would a trusted advisor or therapist suggest you do?

What other information or strategies will help you determine whether it makes sense to invest further in a relationship?

_____

_____

_____

_____

If you decide it's prudent to end a relationship, there's no need to feel guilty. As I've noted throughout this book, the fallacy that all relationships should last forever is not helpful or realistic. Most relationships last for a season, not a lifetime. Put your energy into crafting a plan to leave the relationship safely and with integrity. Also, be sure to prioritize grieving. The end of a relationship—even when you choose it—is still a loss that needs to be mourned. The strategies in chapter 4 can help you do this.

Final Thoughts

In this chapter, we explored how to identify and create healthy relationships, learn to trust, build mutuality, determine our deal-breakers, understand our emotional triggers, and handle unhealthy relationships. Remember, developing healthy relationships is an ongoing process and you may be just getting started. Be patient and continue to learn and practice healthy relationship skills! With a commitment to personal growth and changing the dysfunctional relationship patterns you learned in childhood, I know you'll be able to develop the healthy relationships you deserve and experience the joys of fulfilling, mature relationships.

CHAPTER 10

Maintaining Boundaries

By severing ties with your parents, you've set a necessary and significant boundary. However, that doesn't mean your boundary work is done! Maintaining low- or no-contact boundaries with your parents may be a lifelong process that you'll need to put considerable time and effort into holding (Agllias 2018; Scharp 2014). In addition to draining your emotional energy, maintaining boundaries with parents can be stressful and anxiety provoking (Agllias 2018). This chapter will help you understand the importance of boundaries and common ways that parents and other family members challenge them, and provide tips for maintaining firm boundaries and overcoming barriers that make boundary setting difficult.

Why Boundaries Matter

An interpersonal boundary is a limit that defines who you are as an individual and how you'll interact with others. Boundaries have several purposes (Martin 2021):

- Boundaries keep you safe. They are limits that communicate how you want to be treated and protect you from physical and emotional harm.

- Boundaries differentiate you from others and clarify what you are and aren't responsible for. Your boundaries define you as a separate, autonomous person—not an extension or a clone of your parents. Boundaries allow you to have your own thoughts, feelings, interests, and needs.

- Boundaries help us prioritize what's most important. We all have limited resources, and boundaries ensure that we say yes to people and things that matter and no to those that don't. Otherwise, we may overwork, overspend, overgive, or invest in relationships that don't serve us.

We need boundaries in all relationships. In relationships built on mutual respect and concern for each other's needs, most boundaries can be flexible. However, in dysfunctional relationships, boundaries need to be firm and unwavering because people who behave in immature, toxic, and narcissistic ways do not respect other people's limits; they feel entitled to do whatever they want or are unaware of or indifferent to how their behavior harms others. Boundaries are an essential form of self-protection. Without them, your parents will continue to hurt you.

Violations of Low- and No-Contact Boundaries

The following list contains behaviors that are usually unacceptable to adult children who've set low- or no-contact boundaries with their parents. Although your experiences may be different, this list, and the examples that follow, will help you spot common ways that people challenge boundaries.

- Calling or texting

- Emailing

- Sending letters, cards, or gifts

- Contacting your children or partner

- Sending your children cards or gifts

- Messaging through social media

- Gleaning information about you from your social media profiles and those of your partner or friends

- Creating fake social media accounts to follow or connect with you online

- Gossiping or spreading rumors about you on- or offline, or posting malicious things about you online

- Having a third party contact you or report on your movements

- Driving by your home or workplace

- Showing up at places you frequent, such as your home, church, or children's school

- Dragging out legal proceedings or making it difficult for you to collect an inheritance

> **Gentle Reminder:** Contact from your parents can elicit mixed emotions. You might feel pleased to know they thought of you but also angry or resentful at their repeated manipulations and resistance to honoring your boundaries.

Let's consider some of the boundary challenges Juan and Mina faced after cutting ties with their parents. After reading their stories, you'll have a chance to reflect on your experiences.

• *Juan*

After cutting ties, Juan's mother persisted in trying to contact him. She called and texted him frequently, sometimes late at night, demanding help with one problem or another and trying to make him feel guilty for not assisting. Juan never answered, but seeing her calls and texts was distressing. For his own peace of mind, he blocked her number. His mother then resorted to calling his workplace, showing up unannounced at his home, and attempting to communicate with him and his wife through social media platforms. His mother's behavior caused him to feel anxious. He couldn't concentrate at work, and it strained his relationship with his wife as she too was negatively affected by his mother's intrusive behavior.

• *Mina*

During the first six months of her estrangement, Mina's mother called occasionally to ask Mina to apologize to her father and reconcile. These calls threw her into a tailspin of anger, anxiety, and guilt. She stopped taking her mother's calls, and to her surprise they stopped. However, her mother continued sending gifts to Mina's daughter every holiday—big or small. Mina was angry with her mother for disregarding her request for no contact, and she was concerned about the manipulation and confusion it could cause for her young daughter. Mina emailed her mother and asked her to stop. Her mother responded with a long letter containing an insincere apology and an attempt to shift blame onto Mina for keeping her daughter away from her grandparents. Mina chose not to respond so as not to encourage more contact from her mother. She then heard from extended family members that her mother was spreading rumors, accusing her of being mentally ill and an unfit parent.

Have your experiences been similar to Juan's and Mina's? How so?

_____

_____

_____

_____

_____

_____

Identify one or two specific boundary challenges that you're currently experiencing—or have recently experienced—with your parents or other family members.

_____

_____

_____

_____

_____

_____

How have these experiences impacted you? Consider your mood, overall health and well-being, other relationships, productivity, and so forth.

_____

_____

_____

_____

_____

_____

How might you benefit from maintaining firmer boundaries with your parents or other family members?

_____

_____

_____

_____

_____

_____

The difficulties you've had maintaining boundaries with your parents are not your fault. Enforcing boundaries is much harder with people who don't see you as a competent adult and who actively work against your attempts to limit contact.

Barriers to Maintaining Firm Boundaries

Adult children who grew up in families that don't respect their autonomy and limits often struggle with boundaries. So, it makes sense that setting boundaries may be uncomfortable or frustrating for you. Furthermore, false beliefs, fear, loneliness, guilt, and manipulation can derail your attempts to set and maintain boundaries.

False Beliefs About Boundaries

Many adult children who are estranged from family members suffer unnecessarily because they have false ideas about boundaries. For example, they refuse to block unwanted calls, texts, and emails—or they agonize over doing so and feel guilty about it—because they think it's mean to do so.

What negative beliefs about boundaries do you hold?

☐ Boundaries are mean.

☐ Boundaries are selfish.

☐ Boundaries hurt people.

☐ Boundaries are rude.

☐ Boundaries don't work.

☐ Boundaries _____.

How do these beliefs interfere with your boundary-setting efforts?

_____

_____

_____

_____

_____

Boundaries are not inherently mean, selfish, hurtful, rude, or ineffective. Although these beliefs may feel true, they're false. Some are widely held in Western society, and others you learned from your family of origin to discourage you from setting boundaries. You have the right to protect yourself by setting boundaries and deserve to do so. Use the following reminders (Martin 2021) to help you see boundaries in a more positive light.

Boundaries are:

• Self-care

• Choices that help you feel safe

• Limits that protect your health, safety, and resources

• Statements or actions that express what you need or want

• Part of every healthy relationship

• A personal right

Write a positive statement about boundaries to remind yourself that it's okay to set them.

_____

_____

Fear and Loneliness

Fear and loneliness can also make it difficult to maintain boundaries. For example, Dan answered his mother's calls out of fear. When he saw her name on the caller ID, he'd think *Maybe she's calling to tell me something important, such as Grandma's sick*, and he'd take her calls. And when he was particularly lonely, he'd text his mother or sister, but they never provided the comfort he sought, and in time he strengthened his boundaries and learned to rely on friends or a crisis support line when he felt low. Like Dan, there may be times when you feel lonely, miss your family, or are afraid of missing family updates, which lead you to loosen your boundaries.

How does fear interfere with your boundary setting?

_____

_____

_____

_____

_____

How does loneliness interfere with your boundary setting?

_____

_____

_____

_____

_____

Fear and loneliness indicate that you're hurting and need to treat yourself with compassion. What self-care activities and supportive people can help you cope with fear and loneliness without compromising your boundaries?

_____

_____

_____

_____

_____

Guilt

We feel guilty when we think we've done something wrong, such as not fulfilling our family obligations. Even after cutting ties, you may find that beliefs about how you *should* interact with your family persist and you feel guilty when you don't behave as your family or society expects you to. Then, to relieve feelings of guilt, you may relax your boundaries. Here's an example:

Thought: *I should call my father on his birthday.* → Feeling: *Guilty* → Action: *Call father*

If you have a functional relationship with your father, this sequence of events isn't problematic, and you'll likely feel satisfied or pleased after calling him. However, if you've cut ties due to being mistreated or other dysfunctional dynamics, relieving your guilty feelings by reestablishing a connection typically leads to additional painful emotions and experiences.

How do feelings of guilt make it challenging to hold firm boundaries?

_____

_____

_____

_____

_____

You can alleviate guilty feelings by changing your expectations and remembering that you no longer need to try to please your parents and meet their expectations. You can do this by replacing "should statements" with "choice statements." Here's an example:

Should statement: *I should call my father on his birthday.*

Choice statement: *Calling my father on his birthday—or not—is my choice.*

I choose not to contact my father on his birthday.

Practice writing should statements based on obligations or expectations that cause you to feel guilty. Then, write choice statements that emphasize that you get to decide whether you interact with your family and how you do so.

Should statement: _____

Choice statement: _____

Should statement: _____

Choice statement: _____

Manipulation and Mind Games

Some estranged parents go to great lengths to maintain contact. These parents aren't motivated by love and goodwill but want to control or punish their children. They are effective manipulators who know just what to do to upset you or get you to respond. Mina's story from earlier in this chapter is a good example of this dynamic. Her mother called not because she was interested in her daughter's well-being, but to shift the blame for the estrangement onto Mina and pressure her to apologize. When this didn't work, she disparaged Mina to the rest of the family to cast herself and her husband as the victims of a troubled, disrespectful daughter. Her parents' behavior reflected their refusal to take responsibility for the harm they caused Mina and her child and their need to exert control over her.

Put a checkmark next to the forms of manipulation that you've experienced.

☐ **Gaslighting:** Your parents twist reality or deny what they said or did so that you question your perceptions and memories. For example, your mother tells you that you're overreacting or that an abusive incident never happened.

☐ **Triangulation:** Your parents use a third party to gain access to you or convince you to reconnect. For example, your father texts your spouse when you won't respond or asks your child for your new phone number.

☐ **Guilt trips:** Your parents manipulate your empathy to coerce you into seeing or talking to them or doing things for them. For example, your stepmother tells you that your father's been depressed since you cut ties and that you need to visit or he'll never recover.

☐ **Love-bombing:** Your parents are excessively nice, send gifts or flowers, or apologize to convince you they've changed. For example, your parents want to give you their car so you'll feel indebted to them—not because they want to make your life easier.

How do manipulations and mind games make it challenging for you to hold firm boundaries?

_____

_____

_____

_____

The key to not succumbing to manipulations and mind games is to recognize them for what they are.

How do you know when your parents are trying to manipulate you? What does it sound like? What does it look like? What emotions or bodily sensations do you experience?

_____

_____

_____

_____

_____

If you're unsure, who can help you identify manipulations and mind games?

_____

When you notice that you're being manipulated, name it. Doing so will help you see the situation realistically and maintain self-protective boundaries. I encourage you to name the manipulation and your intention to hold a boundary aloud and write it down for maximum effectiveness.

Example: _My parents are trying to manipulate me. This is a guilt trip; I'm not going to fall for it._

Try writing some of your own.

_____

_____

_____

_____

_____

It's normal to have a strong emotional response to manipulations and mind games. Remember that manipulations are designed to get you to react. Instead, take time to explore your feelings, calm your nervous system, and seek counsel before deciding if or how to respond. You may find it helpful to revisit the Respond Rather Than React exercise you tried in chapter 9.

Gentle Reminder: Reacting with anger to boundary violations may encourage your parents to further challenge your boundaries as it shows them that they can still control you.

Is It Ever Helpful to Respond?

Assessing your parents' motivation for contacting you can be tricky. Certainly, some parents do make genuine attempts to express regret, apologize, or reconcile. However, in my experience as a therapist, this is not always the case. It can be helpful to ask yourself what form of communication would demonstrate the most respect for you and your boundaries. For example, showing up unannounced at my workplace would not indicate to me that someone's considered my feelings and needs, whereas a formal written letter would reflect higher regard for me. What feels respectful to you may be different given your individual experiences, age, and culture. Ultimately, you must do what feels right to you.

Gentle Reminder: You are not obligated to listen or respond to someone just because they contact you.

Some might argue that if you don't respond, you'll never know if your parents have made meaningful changes and are capable of engaging in a respectful, adult relationship. Instead of focusing on your parents and whether they've changed, I encourage you to focus on yourself and what you need. First and foremost, consider how responding is likely to impact your mental health. Will it undo the hard work you've put into your healing? This is generally the case for my clients. There is an increase or return of symptoms that they experienced earlier in their healing process—rumination, anger, insomnia, sadness, guilt, and second-guessing their decision to cut ties—and they report that gains that took months to achieve are undone in minutes. Although this may not be true for everyone, it's important to trust your instincts and be aware of how emotionally strong you feel or how susceptible you are to your parents' efforts to hurt or manipulate you. The next exercise can help you decide whether to read, listen, or respond to correspondence from your parents. You can download additional copies at this book's website, http://www.newharbinger.com/53905, so you can repeat it for different circumstances.

Exercise: Deciding How to Respond

How have your parents tried to contact you?

_____

_____

Do you want to have this type of contact with your parents now? Why or why not?

_____

_____

_____

What do you think will happen if you have contact? Is this outcome realistic based on your experience with and knowledge of your family?

_____

_____

_____

What do you have to gain?

_____

_____

_____

What do you have to lose?

_____

_____

_____

How do you feel about this attempt to contact you?

_____

_____

_____

How might you deal with these feelings without resuming contact?

_____

_____

_____

Are you emotionally prepared to handle being hurt again? What support people and coping skills can you utilize?

_____

_____

_____

Whatever you choose to do about the contact attempt, be gentle with yourself. We all feel uncertain and make mistakes, especially in complex and emotionally charged situations such as these.

Gentle Reminder: Unwanted contact can damage your mental health. You have the right to protect yourself.

Tips for Maintaining Firm Boundaries

The boundaries that you need are unique to you and your situation. These tips are designed to give you general guidance about how to maintain low- or no-contact boundaries and keep yourself safe from intrusive or hurtful contact.

Phone and Online Contact

There is an increasing number of ways that family members can use technology to violate your boundaries. To protect yourself from these forms of contact, consider:

- Blocking the phone numbers and email addresses of your parents and others who don't respect your request for no contact

- Unfriending, unfollowing, or blocking those you don't want to see or hear from on social media

- Blocking mutual friends and family members to prevent your parents from seeing comments or posts that mention you

- Untagging yourself in photos and setting your accounts to limit the tagging capabilities of others

- Using the highest privacy settings available on social media accounts

- Changing your passwords

Technology is constantly changing, and it's not difficult for sneaky and persistent people to find ways to contact you or get information about you online. Be thoughtful about what you share via technology and with whom you share it. Remember, people can screenshot and share with anyone anything you post online or write in an email or text. If you're not technologically savvy, you may want to have a friend help you with your technology use and settings.

What steps do you need to take to strengthen your privacy online and avoid unwanted contact?

_____

_____

_____

_____

_____

> **Gentle Reminder:** Empower yourself to use all boundary-setting tools at your disposal.

Mail and Gifts

You have several options for dealing with unwanted mail and gifts. Most importantly, know that you don't have to open or respond to either. As you read these ideas, notice which ones feel like the right approach for you. You can place a checkmark next to them.

- ☐ Immediately throw away letters or cards without opening them.

- ☐ Put mail in a designated, out-of-the-way place (like a drawer). You can decide to open it or not at a later date.

- ☐ Ask your partner or roommate to screen mail from your parents. Advise them of what circumstances you want to hear about the letter's contents.

- ☐ Read and process mail from your parents with your therapist.

- ☐ Donate gifts to charity.

- ☐ Return mail to the sender.

How will you handle unwanted mail or gifts?

_____

_____

_____

_____

_____

In-Person Encounters

If you live near your parents, it's possible they'll intentionally show up at your home or another place you frequent, or you may randomly run into them at the grocery store or gas station. The specifics of your situation will dictate the best course of action for you; the following ideas can help you outline a plan to manage in-person encounters:

- Leave or keep your distance.

- If you must interact, keep it short and polite; restate your boundaries, if needed.

- Contact law enforcement, if necessary, and explore your legal options, such as getting a restraining order.

- Inform your employer, children's school, or others so they know how to respond to visits from your parents.

- Talk to your partner and children, if appropriate, so you all know how to handle encounters with your parents.

In the past, how have you handled unexpected encounters with your parents?

_____

_____

_____

_____

_____

How would you like to handle them in the future? What steps will help you prepare?

_____

_____

_____

_____

_____

_____

Even if you don't follow this plan exactly, it's helpful to have a plan for managing unexpected contact. In the moment, you may feel anxious or overwhelmed, and it's hard to create an action plan when you're caught off guard.

Final Thoughts

As you work to maintain boundaries with your parents or other family members, remember that boundaries are a fundamental form of self-protection, and we all have the right to safeguard our physical and mental well-being. Maintaining firm boundaries takes a lot of effort. Recognizing and working against barriers to strong boundaries, such as false beliefs, fear, loneliness, guilt, and manipulative behaviors, will help you successfully enforce low- or no-contact boundaries, so you can protect yourself and continue healing. In the next chapter, you'll learn to navigate more of the challenging situations that adult children commonly face after cutting ties.

CHAPTER 11

Coping with Holidays, Special Occasions, and Other Challenging Situations

Holidays, special occasions—even death and dying—typically bring families together. But for adult children who are estranged from their parents and other family members, these events can be painful reminders of the family relationships they no longer have or the love they never received. They present dilemmas about how to deal with societal and family pressures and find new, fulfilling ways to mark these events. This chapter will address ways to cope with holidays, special occasions, and events such as a parent's illness or death, and how to talk to your own children about your estrangement, resolve differing opinions with your partner, and respond to questions about your family of origin.

Holidays and Special Occasions

Holidays and special occasions, such as weddings, births, and graduations, are challenging for many reasons:

- They're emotionally charged.

- They can trigger positive memories and nostalgia.

- They can trigger traumatic memories.

- We have fixed ideas and high expectations about what these events should be like.

- There's strong social pressure to celebrate in particular ways, usually involving a close-knit family.

- It may be hard to avoid contact with your family of origin.

Dan's story shows us how estrangement-related grief can intensify during holidays. After reading about his experiences, reflect on your own.

• Dan

During the first few years of his estrangement, Dan felt a mixture of sadness, loneliness, and relief during the holidays. He had happy memories of the family gatherings of his early childhood. His mother and grandmother taught him to cook, and the family watched football together, played charades, and laughed a lot. He missed the happy times he once had and was lonely, especially when everyone else seemed to be spending time with their families. The depictions of happy families were everywhere—in movies, at shopping malls, and on social media—magnifying his sense of shame and isolation.

What holidays and special occasions have been difficult for you? What events do you anticipate being difficult in the future?

_____

_____

_____

_____

_____

What in particular makes these occasions difficult for you?

_____

_____

_____

_____

_____

Should You Attend?

One of the first questions adult children who are estranged may face regarding holidays and special occasions is whether to have contact with their family of origin. For some, the answer is a definitive no, whereas others may contemplate giving their parents one more chance or feel compelled to celebrate a special event with family despite their parents' presence. Typically, the biggest risk of having contact with your family on holidays or special occasions is that you'll be hurt—again.

> **Gentle Reminder:** Don't assume that your family will treat you well because it's a holiday or special occasion.

You will need to weigh the pros and cons of reengaging with your family and assess whether you have the emotional bandwidth to do so and what healthy coping would entail.

In what circumstances would having contact with your family during a holiday or special occasion be right for you?

_____

_____

_____

_____

_____

What would you hope to gain? Is this realistic?

_____

_____

_____

_____

_____

What would indicate that having contact is not in your best interest?

_____

_____

_____

_____

_____

What risks would contact present?

_____

_____

_____

_____

_____

Please know that choosing not to attend is not a personal failing. Your self-protective boundaries are not the problem. Your parents' mistreatment is the reason your family cannot joyfully celebrate special occasions together. If you choose to attend a family gathering, the following tips can help you prioritize your needs and well-being.

Tips for Attending Family Gatherings

- Arrive and leave early. Being the first to arrive gives you time to get your bearings and ease into the event.

- Have an exit plan. It can be hard to extract oneself from a gathering. So, know how you'll make your exit, what you'll say to the host when you leave, and so forth. You can also let the host know ahead of time that you'll be leaving early; no explanation is necessary.

- Bring a support person, if possible.

- Ask others not to force interactions.

- Take breaks. When you feel overwhelmed or upset, step outside, volunteer to play with the children, or splash water on your face and take some deep breaths in the bathroom.

- Repeat an encouraging mantra in your head such as *I can handle this.*

- Refrain from gossip.

- Excuse yourself from uncomfortable conversations.

> **Gentle Reminder:** When celebrating a special occasion with your family of origin, keep things light and polite.

Whether you see your family of origin or not, holidays and special occasions can still be fraught with complex emotions and societal expectations, and most of us need to find new ways to mark these events while navigating these accompanying emotions and expectations. The next section will help you identify strategies to make holidays and special occasions more manageable.

Thriving During Holidays and Special Occasions

Holidays and special occasions needn't be as painful as they've been in the past. Anticipating and preparing for difficult events, such as whether you'll have contact with your parents or not, will help you handle them more effectively. With self-awareness, practice, and an open mind you'll find strategies that ease your pain—and maybe even restore some of the joy or meaning to these events. Let's return to Dan's story for inspiration.

- *Dan's Strategies*

Amid his grief and loneliness, Dan was relieved not to have to endure his parents' transphobia and rejection. Reminding himself of this helped him weather the challenges of being without a family during the holidays. To reduce his sadness and isolation, Dan actively sought out alternative ways to spend Thanksgiving. Volunteering at a senior living facility gave him a sense of purpose and gratitude. It renewed his belief in the goodness of humanity, and in the process he made new friends. Dan also found relief in participating in a "turkey trot," treating himself to a special meal, and writing in his journal. Now that he's forged close relationships, he celebrates Friendsgiving with his chosen family or travels during the holidays.

Which of Dan's strategies might help you cope with a difficult holiday or special occasion? Or how might you adapt them?

_____

_____

_____

_____

> **Gentle Reminder:** You may need different strategies for different occasions. With practice, you'll find ones that work for you.

The following tips can help you identify additional strategies that may help you cope not only with holidays and other notable events, but also with the days before and after these events, which can be equally challenging. If it's useful, place a checkmark next to those that appeal to you.

Tips for Navigating Difficult Events

- ☐ Acknowledge your feelings and find healthy outlets for them.

- ☐ Seek support. Lean on others for strength and comfort, whether it's professional support or that from friends.

- ☐ Increase self-care before and after the holiday or event. I call this a "self-care sandwich."

- ☐ Avoid social media or anything that stirs up strong negative emotions.

- ☐ Give yourself permission not to celebrate or to celebrate in an unconventional way.

- ☐ Free yourself from family traditions; be creative and start your own meaningful traditions or activities.

- ☐ Spend time with others who are without a family.

- ☐ Plan how you'll spend the difficult day. This may mean doing an alternative activity, seeing family, or a combination of the two. Your plan can be flexible so you can adapt according to your needs and feelings, but a completely unstructured day invites rumination, sorrow, and angst.

Considering your needs and strengths, what additional strategies will you try?

_____

_____

_____

_____

Use the strategies you've identified to create a plan to help you cope with holidays and special events. You don't need to follow the plan exactly. Simply making the plan will boost your confidence and remind you of the variety of coping strategies that you can utilize. You can download this worksheet at this book's website, http://www.newharbinger.com/53905, and create additional coping plans.

Exercise: Coping Plan for Holidays and Special Occasions

Identify a specific challenging holiday or special occasion: _____

What can you do to prepare for this event *before* it happens?

_____

_____

_____

What kind of support do you need? Who can provide it?

_____

_____

_____

How will you process your feelings?

_____

_____

_____

_____

What other forms of self-care might you need?

_____

_____

_____

_____

Identify one or two things you can do to make this holiday or occasion more manageable or enjoyable for yourself.

_____

_____

_____

_____

If you'll be seeing someone you're estranged from, how will you handle it? What boundaries do you need?

_____

_____

_____

_____

If this is a recurring holiday or event, what can you start doing now to create the holiday or event you want in the future? For example, you might seek out a new religious community, brainstorm nontraditional ways to spend a holiday, make friends, or start therapy.

_____

_____

_____

_____

How will you take care of yourself *after* this challenging holiday or event?

_____

_____

_____

_____

Illness or Death

It's common for adult children to worry about how they'll handle a parent's illness or death (Agllias 2018). You might feel anxious about social pressures to see your family or what it would be like to interact with them again. If you don't see them, you might worry that you'll regret not saying goodbye or attending the funeral. In addition, you might be worried that no one will notify you when your parent is dying or has died. Conversely, you may prefer not to know and worry that someone will try to involve you. Although it's hard to predict what the situation will entail and how you'll feel when it occurs, acknowledging your fears or concerns today can help you feel more prepared.

What fears or concerns do you have about your parents becoming ill or dying?

_____

_____

_____

_____

When someone you're estranged from is seriously ill or dies, many difficult and conflicting feelings may surface even if you haven't had contact in years and feel at peace with your decision to sever ties. It's okay to feel relieved or even glad when a person who's hurt you dies. It's also natural to feel sad and angry. You aren't just grieving their death; you're grieving the healthy relationship you never had with them. Their death may be a reminder that they couldn't be the loving parent you needed, they wouldn't acknowledge the harm they caused, they wouldn't apologize, and there was no reconciliation or closure.

> **Gentle Reminder:** A parent's illness or death may be painful and a relief.

Although it may not be possible to work out exactly how you'll handle a family illness or death, thinking through your options now will make it easier for you to cope when the time comes.

Deciding to Have Contact with Your Family in Critical Situations

As we discussed earlier in this chapter, resuming contact with your family, even temporarily, is a risky endeavor. Juan's story demonstrates this.

• *Juan*

Juan received a call from the hospital informing him that his mother was seriously ill. She was being discharged and needed ongoing care at home. Juan was reluctant to get involved but felt obligated as there was no one else to do it. Juan oversaw her daily care, took her to appointments, and managed her medication. Throughout this, his mother was hostile and unappreciative. She often lashed out at Juan, blaming him for her problems and accusing him of abandoning her. After a few weeks, the emotional toll was too great; Juan hired a caregiver for his mother and cut ties once again. He regretted seeing her again.

If you choose to interact with an estranged parent or other family member in an extraordinary circumstance, you must have realistic expectations. Emotions and tensions are typically high in these situations—even in well-functioning families. Unless you have concrete evidence of a transformation, assume your family members will treat you as they have in the past. With this in mind, don't expect:

- An apology or deathbed confession

- Contact will bring closure

- Contact will heal old wounds

- Contact will alleviate guilty feelings

- Your family will be happy to hear from or see you

- Your family will appreciate your contributions

There may be instances when resuming contact with an ill parent or attending a memorial feels like the right choice. When Dan's mother died, he opted to attend her funeral largely because he received a heartfelt invitation from his sister. He did not feel a need to publicly mourn or remember his mother. However, it was an opportunity to reconnect with his sister, and after speaking to her he felt hopeful about potentially mending their relationship.

In what circumstances would having contact with an ill parent or attending a memorial service be right for you?

_____

_____

_____

_____

What would you hope to gain? Is this realistic?

_____

_____

_____

_____

_____

What would indicate that having contact isn't in your best interest?

_____

_____

_____

_____

_____

In addition to having realistic expectations, Dan went to the funeral with clarity about his boundaries and goals. He knew the interactions would be strained and emotionally draining, so he decided ahead of time what he'd do and not do. For him, it helped to keep the visit short and limit what he shared about himself. If you choose to have contact with your family, be clear with yourself about what that entails. Understanding your boundaries and goals will help you maintain emotional safety and know when to engage further and when to retreat. It's difficult to set these parameters until the situation arises. So, I encourage you to return to the following questions as needed:

- What's the purpose of having contact?

- What forms of contact will you have (phone, text, email, in person)?

- Who will you have contact with? Who will you not have contact with?

- Will contact be a one-time occurrence (such as attending a memorial) or for the duration of the situation (illness, settling the estate, cleaning out your parents' house, for example)?

Deciding Not to Have Contact with Your Family in Critical Situations

Firstly, know that you are not obligated to contact your parents or family when someone is ill or has died. It's not your job to take care of people who've mistreated you or to forgive or reconcile with your parents so they can die peacefully. As an emotionally mature adult, it's your job to take care of yourself. As we've discussed throughout this book, maintaining self-protective boundaries is a fundamental way to do this.

Mina had good reasons for cutting ties with her parents, and that didn't change when her father became ill. As you read her story, notice her reasons for not visiting and what feelings they evoke in you.

• *Mina*

Mina's mother notified her that her father had cancer and his death was imminent. She begged Mina to visit for a last chance to apologize to her father and "make things right." Mina politely declined, not explaining why, as she knew her mother would argue and pick apart her reasons. Mina knew this was the right choice. She had nothing to say to her father and wanted nothing from him, nor did she want to get entangled in her mother's manipulative behavior. Mina had moved on, and seeing her parents again would have been a step backward.

What aspects of Mina's experience resonate with you?

_____

_____

_____

How did you feel reading Mina's story?

_____

_____

_____

How will you know that maintaining no contact is the right choice when a parent is ill or has died? Consider what information, thoughts, feelings, or physical symptoms would inform your decision.

_____

_____

_____

_____

_____

Damned If You Do and Damned If You Don't

No matter what you do, you may feel uncertain or anxious about your choices. There's also a good chance that you'll be misunderstood or judged by those around you. Friends and acquaintances who have healthy relationships with their parents are unlikely to understand your dilemma and feelings. Conventional grief support may not fit your needs if it assumes that you miss or feel sad about your parent's death. Having conflicting feelings and a complicated relationship with the deceased is not uncommon, but it's often hard for people to acknowledge and talk about feeling angry or relieved that a family member has died. Do your best to seek support from those who can empathize, and know that you should do what's best for your mental health even if others don't understand.

How can you stay true to yourself even if others misunderstand or judge your choices?

_____

_____

_____

_____

Other Challenging Situations

In addition to holidays, special occasions, illness, and death, you may find it challenging to talk to others, including your children, about your estrangement and deal with a partner's differing opinion about contact with your family of origin. This section offers guidance on these matters.

Talking to Your Children About Estrangement

How do you explain family estrangement to your children? What should you tell them about their grandparents? When should you tell them? These are valid questions, and although there aren't easy answers, these tips can help you determine what's best for your children.

- **Keep it simple.** In a developmentally appropriate way, explain why you don't have contact with your parents. Keep it short and simple for younger children and share more with older children. Rarely is it helpful to give children—even adult children—a detailed accounting of all the ways your family harmed you. You don't want to burden them with information that they aren't emotionally mature enough to handle. Doing so can frighten, confuse, or upset them.

- **Be clear that it's not their fault.** Young children, especially those under age eight, cannot comprehend the complexities of adult relationships and may mistakenly believe they are responsible. Therefore, it's important to explicitly tell them that they didn't cause the estrangement and are not responsible for it.

- **Explain what's changing.** Tell your children what will change in their lives due to estrangement. Mention specific events or interactions that won't happen anymore, such as "We won't be going to Nana's birthday dinner."

- **Acknowledge their feelings.** Validate your children's emotions and let them know that it's okay to feel sad and miss their grandparents and to be angry—even at you. Help them find healthy ways to express their feelings, such as through art, writing, play, or movement.

- **Have an open dialogue.** Treat the subject as an ongoing conversation. As your children mature, they may need more information and a deeper understanding of the situation and issues involved, such as healthy relationships, trauma, and addiction. Invite them to ask questions, and be open to answering them. This builds trust between you and your children and signals that it's safe to talk about sensitive subjects.

- **Give older teens more autonomy.** If your teenager wants to continue a relationship with people you're estranged from, and doing so doesn't endanger them, consider their request. Understandably this may be painful for you. Remember, your goal is to keep your children safe, not to control them; trying to control older children and who they have relationships with can backfire. Perhaps another supportive adult can facilitate or monitor your children's relationship with your family of origin so that you can remain removed.

> **Gentle Reminder:** How you approach talking to your children will depend on their developmental level, their personality or temperament, whether they had a relationship with the family members you've cut ties with, and whether there are any ongoing safety concerns involving your children.

What aspects of your children's developmental level, personalities, strengths, and challenges will guide how you talk with them about your estrangement?

_____

_____

_____

_____

_____

Use the space below to start formulating a script for your initial—or next—conversation with your children about your family of origin.

_____

_____

_____

_____

_____

_____

_____

_____

Who might help you determine the best approach to talking with your children?

_____

Gentle Reminder: Let your children know that family isn't limited to blood relations. Help them notice nontraditional families among their friends, in books, and on television.

Your Partner Wants to Stay in Touch with Your Family

If your partner expresses interest in maintaining a relationship with your family of origin, you may feel hurt, angry, or defensive; such a request can be very painful because it minimizes or invalidates the harm your family caused you. Although it's challenging, don't assume that your partner lacks empathy. Be curious about their reasons for wanting contact with your family. Perhaps they don't fully understand what transpired between you and your parents, or they want your children to have a relationship with their grandparents. In my experience, it's hard for folks who grew up in functional families to understand how cruel some parents can be. You need to be vulnerable enough to share your story such that your partner understands your rationale. And your partner needs to listen with an open mind and trusting heart.

Gentle Reminder: A safe partner wants to understand your past so they can support you in the present.

When you and your partner understand each other's needs and wants regarding contact with your family, you can jointly find alternate ways to meet those needs or wants. For example, if your partner wants to be a part of big family celebrations because his family is small, you can explore other ways to accomplish or approximate this. Answering the following questions with your partner will help you get started. If you reach an impasse, or emotions are so strong that communication breaks down, individual or couples therapy may be helpful.

Why does your partner want to maintain contact with your family of origin?

_____

_____

_____

_____

_____

What are some alternate ways to accomplish this or address their concerns?

_____

_____

_____

_____

_____

Handling Questions About Your Family of Origin

Navigating questions about your family of origin from colleagues, neighbors, and acquaintances can also be stressful. Naturally, your responses will vary depending on who's asking, and what and why it's being asked. Take a moment to think about your approach thus far.

How have you handled questions about family members you're estranged from?

_____

_____

_____

_____

_____

What about this approach has worked? What hasn't worked?

_____

_____

_____

_____

_____

In an effort to be polite, you may feel obliged to offer more information than you feel comfortable sharing. However, not everyone needs or deserves to know the details of your family relationships and trauma. Having a simple statement prepared for such occasions can help alleviate the pressure you may feel. Here are some examples:

- I don't have a relationship with my parents.

- I won't be seeing my family over the holidays. We're no longer on speaking terms.

- My parents were difficult [not supportive, or some other phrase], and I've distanced myself from them.

- That's a sensitive subject. Let's talk about something else.

Try writing a few statements of your own.

_____

_____

_____

Gentle Reminder: You don't have to share personal information just because someone asks.

Final Thoughts

Although family estrangement presents numerous challenges, identifying and practicing coping strategies will give you the skills and confidence to handle them. With continued practice, you'll move from simply getting through these challenges to thriving—freeing yourself from social pressures and feeling good about doing what's right for you. In the conclusion, we'll review the most impactful strategies for healing and thriving after cutting ties, and I'll share some tips to help you persevere when recovery feels overwhelming.

Continuing to Grow

We've covered a lot of ground in this workbook—and you should be proud of the time and effort you've invested in your recovery! It's completely normal to still be struggling. Healing from childhood trauma and family estrangement is a process, one that's often slower than we'd like. We'll use this concluding chapter to review your progress, find meaning, identify areas for continued growth, and plan for inevitable setbacks.

Notice Your Progress

We addressed three areas of growth in this book: acceptance, healing, and thriving. Because change is incremental, we don't always recognize how far we've come. Look back through the chapters and notice what you learned and how it has helped you move forward.

Part 1: Acceptance

What did you learn about accepting your decision to cut ties? Which concepts and exercises resonated with you?

_____

_____

_____

_____

_____

_____

_____

How did you grow or change as a result of having worked through part 1?

_____

_____

_____

_____

_____

_____

_____

_____

Part 2: Healing

What did you learn about healing? Which concepts and exercises resonated with you?

_____

_____

_____

_____

_____

_____

_____

_____

How did you grow or change as a result of having worked through part 2?

_____

_____

_____

_____

_____

_____

_____

_____

Part 3: Thriving

What did you learn about thriving? Which concepts and exercises resonated with you?

_____

_____

_____

_____

_____

_____

_____

How did you grow or change as a result of having worked through part 3?

_____

_____

_____

_____

_____

_____

_____

Find Meaning

We can build resilience by finding meaning in painful experiences and reframing them as opportunities for empowerment and growth (Linden and Sillence 2021). This process is known as "meaning making," "benefit finding," or "post-traumatic growth." It's a continuous process and not something most of us can do until we've soothed the raw emotions that accompany estrangement. As you heal, see if you can find the silver lining or lessons learned that have improved your life since cutting ties. Finding meaning doesn't mean you *want* to be estranged or that your pain isn't real, it's choosing to focus on what's working in your life rather than on what's wrong or lacking. Here are a few examples.

Juan: *I finally feel loved and supported. My chosen family has shown me what family really means.*

Mina: *I'm not controlling like my parents. I let my daughter make her own choices.*

Dan: *I can relax and be myself. I can pursue my goals.*

What is the silver lining of having cut ties with your parents?

_____

_____

_____

_____

_____

_____

How have you grown as a person through the processes of estrangement and healing?

_____

_____

_____

_____

_____

_____

Set Goals

Coping with family estrangement is ongoing, and it's not realistic to expect that, having done the work of this book, you've overcome all of its challenges. With this in mind, think about what areas of your recovery need more attention.

What are your long-term goals (one to two years) for growth and recovery?

_____

_____

_____

_____

_____

What are your short-term goals (six to twelve months) for growth and recovery?

_____

_____

_____

_____

_____

How will you know when you've achieved them? How will you feel? How will your life be different?

_____

_____

_____

_____

_____

Who and what will help you reach these goals?

_____

_____

_____

_____

_____

_____

Stay Motivated

Everyone feels discouraged at times. This is especially true for people coping with family estrangement because friends and communities often don't understand it and there aren't many support services available that deal with it specifically. When you experience a setback, try these tips:

- Intentionally practice what's worked in the past. Sometimes, we get complacent, or life circumstances disrupt healthy habits and coping strategies that support our healing and thriving. Being diligent about incorporating them into your daily activities can get you back on track.

- Adjust when needed. If the strategies you're using aren't effective, try something new. Revisit topics and exercises in this book, listen to podcasts, read articles, and ask your support network for ideas.

- Seek support. Feeling discouraged can be a sign that you need support. You don't need to go through this alone! In addition to your personal support network, use the support resources listed in the appendix.

- Be kind to yourself. When you're struggling, give yourself the same love and grace that you'd give a dear friend. This can be in the form of encouraging words, physical touch, self-care activities, a small gift, or anything else you find comforting.

What emotions, physical signs, or behaviors are indications that your motivation is slipping?

_____

_____

_____

_____

What might help you overcome a setback?

_____

_____

_____

_____

Final Thoughts

Congratulations on completing this workbook! You've taken a huge step toward reclaiming your life. And while you'll encounter challenges along the way, I'm certain you have the skills and confidence you need to handle them. I encourage you to revisit the concepts and exercises in this workbook as part of your ongoing healing process. Using what you've learned, you'll be able to free yourself from toxic family connections and live an authentic, fulfilling life that's enriched by supportive, healthy relationships.

Acknowledgments

Many thanks to…

The editors and staff at New Harbinger for their expert guidance, and for the opportunity to give voice to adult children's experiences, support their healing, and help destigmatize family estrangement.

Allen, Kara, Michelle, Travis, and my writing group for their encouragement, feedback, and accountability.

My clients and all of the adult children who've shared their most vulnerable stories with me. Their experiences showed me unequivocally that cutting ties with one's parents can be a healthy choice, and that healing and thriving are possible!

Support Resources

Additional resources are listed on my website: https://livewellwithsharonmartin.com/family-estrangement -resources

Estrangement Support

Stand Alone: https://www.standalone.org.uk

Together Estranged: https://www.togetherestranged.org

Therapist Directories

Inclusive Therapists: https://www.inclusivetherapists.com

Latinx Therapy: https://latinxtherapy.com

Melanin and Mental Health: https://www.melaninandmentalhealth.com

National Queer and Trans Therapists of Color Network: https://nqttcn.com/en

Neurodivergent Therapists: https://ndtherapists.com

Open Path Psychotherapy Collective (lower-cost counseling): https://openpathcollective.org

Psychology Today: https://www.psychologytoday.com

Therapy Den: https://www.therapyden.com

Therapy for Black Girls: https://providers.therapyforblackgirls.com

Trauma Therapist Network: https://traumatherapistnetwork.com/therapists

Hotlines

988 Suicide and Crisis Lifeline: 988 or 1-800-273-8255

Blackline (Black, Indigenous, People of Color, and LGBTQ+ affirming): 1-800-604-5841

Crisis Text Line: Text HOME to 741741

Trans Lifeline: 1-877-565-8860

Trevor Project Lifeline (LGBTQ+ young people): 1-866-488-7386

12-Step Groups

Adult Children of Alcoholics and Dysfunctional Families World Service Organization: https://adultchildren .org

Al-Anon: https://al-anon.org

Co-Dependents Anonymous: https://coda.org

Essential Truths for Adults Who've Cut Ties with Their Parents

- I am a good person even if I don't have a relationship with my parents.

- It's healthy to protect and care for myself.

- It's okay to prioritize my health and happiness above family relationships.

- My family of origin is not my only or most important family. I can create a family of my choosing.

- I have a right to pursue my goals and interests and live according to my values.

- I do not need to maintain a relationship with people who are cruel or disrespectful.

- Cutting ties is an act of self-preservation, not a way to punish my family of origin.

- I deserve happiness and healing.

- I am not responsible for breaking up my family.

- My family of origin's inability to love and accept me is not a result of there being anything wrong with me. I am lovable.

- My family of origin does not determine my worth.

- I have a right to make my own choices and decide what's best for me.

References

Agllias, K. 2011. "No Longer on Speaking Terms: The Losses Associated with Family Estrangement at the End of Life." *Families in Society: The Journal of Contemporary Social Services* 92: 107–13.

———. 2016. "Disconnection and Decision-Making: Adult Children Explain Their Reasons for Estranging from Parents." *Australian Social Work* 69: 92–104.

———. 2018. "Missing Family: The Adult Child's Experience of Parental Estrangement." *Journal of Social Work Practice* 32: 59–72.

Allen, J. A., and J. Moore. 2017. "Troubling the Functional/Dysfunctional Family Binary Through the Articulation of Functional Family Estrangement." *Western Journal of Communication* 81: 281–99.

Arnold, C. L. 2014. *Small Move, Big Change: Using Microresolutions to Transform Your Life Permanently.* New York: Penguin Books.

Blake, L. 2017. "Parents and Children Who Are Estranged in Adulthood: A Review and Discussion of the Literature." *Journal of Family Theory and Review* 9: 521–36.

Blake, L., B. Bland, and H. Gilbert. 2022. "The Efficacy of a Facilitated Support Group Intervention to Reduce the Psychological Distress of Individuals Experiencing Family Estrangement." *Evaluation and Program Planning* 95: 102–68.

Boss, P. 1999. *Ambiguous Loss: Learning to Live with Unresolved Grief.* Cambridge, MA: Harvard University Press.

———. 2006. *Loss, Trauma, and Resilience: Therapeutic Work with Ambiguous Loss.* New York: W. W. Norton.

Brach, T. 2019. *Radical Compassion: Learning to Love Yourself and Your World with the Practice of RAIN.* New York: Viking.

Breines, J. G., and S. Chen. 2012. "Self-Compassion Increases Self-Improvement Motivation." *Personality and Social Psychology Bulletin* 38: 1133–43.

Campbell, S. 2022. *Adult Survivors of Toxic Family Members: Tools to Maintain Boundaries, Deal with Criticism, and Heal from Shame After Ties Have Been Cut.* Oakland, CA: New Harbinger Publications.

Carastathis, G. S., L. Cohen, E. Kaczmarek, and P. Chang. 2017. "Rejected by Family for Being Gay or Lesbian: Portrayals, Perceptions, and Resilience." *Journal of Homosexuality* 64: 289–320.

Carr, K., A. Holman, J. S. Abetz, J. K. Kellas, and E. Vagnoni. 2015. "Giving Voice to the Silence of Family Estrangement: Comparing Reasons of Estranged Parents and Adult Children in a Nonmatched Sample." *Journal of Family Communication* 15: 130–40.

Conti, R. P. 2015. "Family Estrangement: Establishing a Prevalence Rate." *Journal of Psychology and Behavioral Science* 3: 28–35.

Doka, K. J. 1989. *Disenfranchised Grief: Recognizing Hidden Sorrow.* Lanham, MD: Lexington Books.

Dorrance Hall, E. 2018. "The Communicative Process of Resilience for Marginalized Family Members." *Journal of Social and Personal Relationships* 35: 307–28.

Hill, C. A., and C. J. Gunderson. 2015. "Resilience of Lesbian, Gay, and Bisexual Individuals in Relation to Social Environment, Personal Characteristics, and Emotion Regulation Strategies." *Psychology of Sexual Orientation and Gender Diversity* 2: 232–52.

Holt-Lunstad, J., T. B. Smith, M. Baker, T. Harris, and D. Stephenson. 2015. "Loneliness and Social Isolation as Risk Factors for Mortality: A Meta-Analytic Review." *Perspectives on Psychological Science* 10: 227–37.

Hope, N., R. Koestner, and M. Milyavskaya. 2014. "The Role of Self-Compassion in Goal Pursuit and Well-Being Among University Freshmen." *Self and Identity* 13: 579–93.

Linden, A. H., and E. Sillence. 2021. "'I'm Finally Allowed to Be Me': Parent-Child Estrangement and Psychological Wellbeing." *Families, Relationships and Societies* 10: 325–41.

Lubben, J., M. Gironda, E. Sabbath, J. Kong, and C. Johnson. 2015. "Social Isolation Presents a Grand Challenge for Social Work." *Grand Challenges for Social Work Initiative* 7. https://grandchallengesforsocialwork.org/wp-content/uploads/2015/12/WP7-with-cover.pdf.

Martin, S. 2019. *The CBT Workbook for Perfectionism: Evidence-Based Skills to Help You Let Go of Self-Criticism, Build Self-Esteem, and Find Balance.* Oakland, CA: New Harbinger Publications.

———. 2021. *The Better Boundaries Workbook: A CBT-Based Program to Help You Set Limits, Express Your Needs, and Create Healthy Relationships.* Oakland, CA: New Harbinger Publications.

Melvin, K., and J. Hickey. 2021. "The Changing Impact and Challenges of Familial Estrangement." *The Family Journal: Counseling and Therapy for Couples and Families* 30: 348–56.

Miyagawa, Y., Y. Niiya, and J. Taniguchi. 2020. "When Life Gives You Lemons, Make Lemonade: Self-Compassion Increases Adaptive Beliefs About Failure." *Journal of Happiness Studies* 21: 2051–68.

Mynard, S. 2020. "Experiences of Counselling and Therapy Post Estrangement from Abusive Parents." Master's thesis. University of Northampton, PA.

Neff, K., and C. Germer. 2018. *The Mindful Self-Compassion Workbook: A Proven Way to Accept Yourself, Build Inner Strength, and Thrive.* New York: Guilford Press.

Pillemer, K. 2020. *Fault Lines: Fractured Families and How to Mend Them.* New York: Avery.

Rittenour, C., S. Kromka, S. Pitts, M. Thorwart, J. Vickers, and K. Whyte. 2018. "Communication Surrounding Estrangement: Stereotypes, Attitudes, and (Non)Accommodation Strategies." *Behavioral Sciences* 8: 96–112.

Scharp, K. M. 2014. "(De)Constructing Family: Exploring Communicative Practices in Accomplishing and Maintaining Estrangement Between Adult Children and Their Parents." PhD dissertation. University of Iowa.

———. 2016. "Parent-Child Estrangement: Conditions for Disclosure and Perceived Social Network Member Reactions." *Family Relations* 65: 688–700.

Scharp, K. M., and E. Dorrance Hall. 2017. "Family Marginalization, Alienation, and Estrangement: Questioning the Nonvoluntary Status of Family Relationships." *Annals of the International Communication Association* 41: 28–45.

Scharp, K. M., and L. J. Thomas. 2016. "Family 'Bonds': Making Meaning of Parent-Child Relationships in Estrangement Narratives." *Journal of Family Communication* 16: 32–50.

Scharp, K. M., L. J. Thomas, and C. G. Paxman. 2015. "'It Was the Straw That Broke the Camel's Back': Exploring the Distancing Processes Communicatively Constructed in Parent-Child Estrangement Backstories." *Journal of Family Communication* 15: 330–48.

Stand Alone. 2014. *The Prevalence of Family Estrangement.* https://www.standalone.org.uk/wp-content/uploads/2013/08/StandAlonePrevalenceRESEARCH3.pdf.

Stand Alone and University of Cambridge. 2015. *Hidden Voices: Family Estrangement in Adulthood.* https://www.standalone.org.uk/wp-content/uploads/2015/12/HiddenVoices.FinalReport.pdf.

Worden, J. W. 2009. *Grief Counseling and Grief Therapy: A Handbook for the Mental Health Practitioner,* 4th ed. New York: Springer.

Zhang, J. W., and S. Chen. 2016. "Self-Compassion Promotes Personal Improvement from Regret Experiences via Acceptance." *Personality and Social Psychology Bulletin* 42: 244–58.

Sharon Martin, DSW, LCSW, is a licensed psychotherapist specializing in helping adult children recover from difficult childhoods. She writes extensively about codependency, perfectionism, and healthy relationships, including the popular blog: *Conquering Codependency* for *Psychology Today*. In addition, she is author of *The CBT Workbook for Perfectionism* and *The Better Boundaries Workbook*.

MORE BOOKS from
NEW HARBINGER PUBLICATIONS

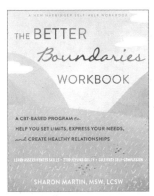

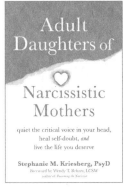

Did you know there are **free tools** you can download for this book?

Free tools are things like **worksheets, guided meditation exercises**, and **more** that will help you get the most out of your book.

You can download free tools for this book—whether you bought or borrowed it, in any format, from any source—from the New Harbinger website. All you need is a NewHarbinger.com account. Just use the URL provided in this book to view the free tools that are available for it. Then, click on the "download" button for the free tool you want, and follow the prompts that appear to log in to your NewHarbinger.com account and download the material.

You can also save the free tools for this book to your **Free Tools Library** so you can access them again anytime, just by logging in to your account! Just look for this button on the book's free tools page. ➜ **+ Save this to my free tools library**

If you need help accessing or downloading free tools, visit **newharbinger.com/faq** or contact us at **customerservice@newharbinger.com**.